You are respectfully invited
to return this book to
Gordon C. Fowler

to DAD

from LOVO
JIM

Travellers in Time

SEVEN EPIC STORIES OF EARLY EXPLORATION

Travellers in Time

SEVEN EPIC STORIES OF EARLY EXPLORATION

COMPILED AND EDITED BY RICHARD ROBINSON
in association with John Robinson and Eric Davidson

Macdonald
Queen Anne Press

A Queen Anne Press BOOK

Introductory and additional editorial material © Richard Robinson 1986
This anthology © Queen Anne Press 1986

First published in Great Britain in 1986 by
Queen Anne Press, a division of
Macdonald & Co (Publishers) Ltd
3rd Floor
Greater London House
Hampstead Road
London NW1 7 QX

A BPCC plc Company

Jacket photographs
Front: from *Pearls and Savages*
Back: from *The Assault on Mount Everest 1922*

British Library Cataloguing in Publication Data
Travellers in time : seven epic stories of
  early exploration.
  1. Discoveries (in geography)   2. Voyages
  and travels
  I. Robinson, Richard
  910′.92′2   G80

  ISBN 0-356-12798-2

Typeset by Acorn Bookwork, Salisbury, Wilts.
Printed and bound in Great Britain by
Hazell, Watson & Viney Limited
Member of the BPCC Group
Aylesbury, Bucks.

Contents

To all who travel hopefully – past, present and future

Introduction

Imagine climbing Mount Everest in a Norfolk jacket, plus-fours and a trilby – like the travellers in 'Everest – The First Attempt: 1922': or flying over the jungles of Papua New Guinea in an aeroplane made of wood and canvas, with the canvas rotting off – as happens in 'Pearls and Savages, 1925': or living in an ice catacombe under the snow, and getting rid of the lice in the reindeer-skin sleeping bag by putting it outside the 'front-door', and so freezing the lice to death – the method adopted in 'Across Greenland by Sledge, 1930'.

Yet to the early time-travellers these incidents were just part of the daily routine – a minor inconvenience in an heroic endeavour: and if their quaint costumes and primitive machines at first provoke a smile – soon the sheer scale of their achievements commands respect: not just how did they do it *then* – but how could anyone do it at any time?

True, they did live in a golden age of exploration – perhaps the last golden age. There were still plenty of 'firsts' to be achieved; to fly a single-engine aircraft from Croyden to Capetown must, in 1925, have seemed almost as difficult – if not impossible – as putting a man on the moon looks later. And there were still a good number of areas on the map marked 'Unknown': so just where and what was the extent of the vast and mysterious continent of Antarctica? The man who in 'Home of the Blizzard' went to find out could exultantly write: 'The sun shone gloriously in a blue sky as we stepped ashore on a charming ice-quay – the first to set foot on the Antarctic continent in a distance of about two thousand miles'.

But there was a high price to be paid for such boldness: two men would never return from Antarctica; in 'Storm, Cape Horn' the author saw the belongings of a seaman lost overboard on the last voyage being brought ashore as he joined the ship. In Greenland frost-bitten toes were amputated without anaesthetic. . . . Such were the hazards – and the rewards – encountered by the characters in *Travellers in Time*, characters who with the passage of the years now look even larger than life, and twice as adventurous. Yet they remain human, warm and even amusing in the midst of their perils.

Here then are seven true stories of adventure, excitement and achievement: of time-travel on a truly epic scale: a scale we cannot help but admire and envy, but can hardly hope to emulate.

Assault on Everest

'We do not live and eat to make money. We eat and make money to be able to enjoy life. Some of us know that by climbing a mountain we can get some of the finest enjoyment there is to be had. The mountain has lifted us, just for one precious moment, high above our ordinary life and shown us the beauty, austerity, power and purity we should never have known if we had not faced the mountain squarely.' Thus declared Brigadier General C. G. Bruce, the commander of the 1922 Everest expedition.

The first attempt to climb the 29,002 feet of Mount Everest, in 1922, was preceded, in 1921, by a reconnaissance expedition led by Colonel Howard Bury and including George Leigh-Mallory, Major Morshead and Captain Wheeler. Its purpose was not only to map the mountain itself, but also the country from Darjeeling to the base camp at the foot of the Rongbuk glacier through which supplies would have to be carried before climbing even began. Until then, no European had been within sixty miles of the base of Everest. As a result of the 1921 survey, it was decided to make a wholehearted attempt on the ascent in the following year.

Amongst the mass of decisions to be taken, there was one which raised considerable controversy: the use of oxygen by the climbers. Those who opposed it believed that whatever beneficial effects it might have, in terms of greater physical strength, would be more than cancelled out by the added weight of the steel cylinders which would have to be carried by the climber. There was also the difficulty of transporting these cylinders across Tibet then up the mountain to the higher camps. A further point against oxygen was that should a climber using it reach a height where the air was thin, and then, by an accident, be suddenly deprived of its use, he would be in a very much worse state than someone who had become gradually acclimatised. The arguments in its favour were that its use would more than compensate for the extra weight, and that not only would the physical strength of the climber be kept closer to normal, but also his mental processes and, above all, his determination would be preserved. It was decided therefore that the 1922 expedition should use oxygen, and the subsequent accounts of the three attempts to reach the summit of Everest, two using oxygen and one, the first, without would seem to show that this decision was correct.

With this difficulty overcome, the expedition assembled at Darjeeling in March 1922. General Bruce's main task was to see that the 'cavalcade' of three hundred baggage animals, twenty ponies, one hundred Tibetan porters, as well as the climbing expedition itself, reached the Base camp safely. This necessitated dealing with the tribal and religious leaders through whose lands the expedition passed, observing their religious customs and avoiding giving offence. Three brief extracts from his account of the journey will give some insight into this side of his work. 'The great Lama of Shekar is an extremely cunning person and a first class trader. We saw a great deal too much of the Lamas of Shekar.' 'The ordinary Dzongpen only has a ceremonial bath on New Year's Eve, and I should not be at all surprised if Mrs Dzongpen didn't too.' But of the Rongbuk Lama Bruce wrote: 'Since he was not a materialist, the question "what is the good of exploring Everest?" was very much easier to answer for him than it was in England.' Bruce found that throughout his journey a Homburg hat was a much coveted present, so he carried a supply with him and found they helped friendly relations greatly. One constant difficulty was finding sufficient fuel. For the climb itself, primus stoves, alcohol stoves and solid fuel 'Metabars' were used, but for the expedition crossing Tibet, local fuel had to be found and there was only one 'local fuel' —

dried yak dung. There were no trees or even bushes for most of the way, and when a patch of bush was discovered, at one point, it had 'devils' in it and had to be left alone.

However, by May 1922 the Base camp was established at the bottom of the Rongbuk glacier, the Tibetans were paid off and the members of the expedition were left alone to start the process of establishing the first three camps up the mountainside. These were spaced at roughly four hours travel apart. Camp I was at 17,800 feet, Camp II at 19,800 feet and Camp III at 21,000 feet. Bad weather slowed work at this stage and Bruce was told it was caused by the services held in Rongbuk monastery which always irritated the demons in the mountain, who tried to stop them by roaring more than usually loud. The services ceased on May 17 and so did the bad weather. It was this same spell of bad weather that caused fears of an early monsoon, and since the oxygen equipment was not yet ready, the decision was taken to allow four members to make an attempt on the summit without it, in case this should be the only opportunity that offered. What follows are the accounts of the leaders of the three teams who tried to climb Everest in that brief spell before the monsoon broke in earnest.

General Bruce and other members of the expedition at the hill camp in Darjeeling

THE EVEREST EXPEDITION, 1922, by Brigadier General the Hon C. G. Bruce, George Leigh-Mallory and Captain George Finch

PREFACE TO THE ASCENT by Brigadier General Bruce

We pitched our camp just below the monastery with considerable difficulty, as the wind was howling rather more than usual. Then we went up to pay our respects to the Rongbuk Lama. This particular Lama was beyond question a remarkable individual. He was a large, well-made man of about sixty, full of dignity, with a most intelligent and wise face and an extraordinarily attractive smile. He was treated with the utmost respect by the whole of his people. (This Lama has the distinction of being actually the incarnation of a god, the god Chongraysay.) We were received with full ceremony.

The Lama's inquiries about the objects of the Expedition were very intelligent, although at the same time they were very difficult to answer. Indeed, this is not strange when one comes to think how many times in England one has been asked, What is the good of an exploration of Everest? What can you get out of it? And, in fact, what is the object generally

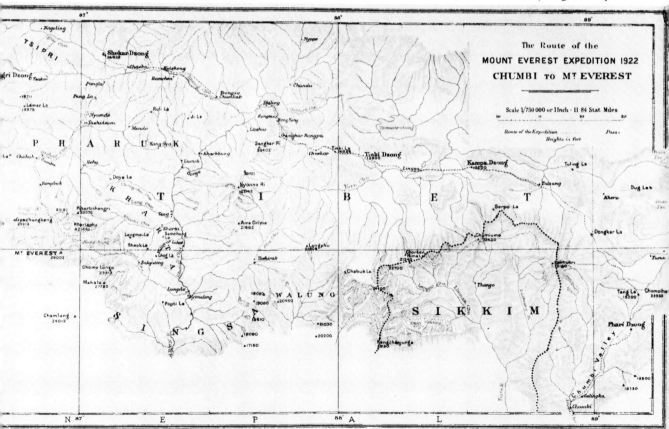

Map of the route followed by the 1922 Everest expedition

of wandering in the mountains? As a matter of fact, it was very much easier to answer the Lama than it is to answer inquiries in England. The Tibetan Lama, especially of the better class, is certainly not a materialist. I was fortunately inspired to say that we regarded the whole Expedition, and especially our attempt to reach the summit of Everest, as a pilgrimage. I am afraid, also, I rather enlarged on the importance of the vows taken by all members of the Expedition.

At any rate, these gentle 'white lies' were very well received, and even my own less excusable one which I uttered to save myself from the dreadful imposition of having to drink Tibetan tea was also sufficiently well received. I told the Lama, through Paul, our interpreter, who, fortunately enough, was able to repress his smiles (an actual record for Paul, which must have strained him to his last ounce of strength), that I had sworn never to touch butter until I had arrived at the summit of Everest. Even this was well received. After that time I drank tea with sugar or milk which was made specially for me.

A word about Tibetan tea: the actual tea from which it is originally made is probably quite sufficiently good, but it is churned up in a great churn with many other ingredients, including salt, nitre, and butter, and the butter is nearly invariably rancid, that is, as commonly made in Tibet. I believe a superior quality is drunk by the upper classes, but at any rate, to the ordinary European taste, castor-oil is pleasant in comparison.

The Lama finally blessed us and blessed our men, and gave us his best wishes for success. As a matter of fact, I really think that the Rongbuk Lama had a friendly feeling for me personally, as he told the interpreter, Karma Paul, that he had discovered that in a previous incarnation I had been a Tibetan Lama. I do not know exactly how to take this. According to the life you lead during any particular incarnation, so are you ranked for the next incarnation; that is to say, if your life has been terrible, down you go to the lowest depths, and as you acquire merit in any particular existence, so in the next birth you get one step nearer to Nirvana. I am perfectly certain that he would consider a Tibetan Lama a good bit nearer the

The chief lama of Rongbuk monastery

right thing than a Britisher could ever be, and so possibly he may have meant that I had not degenerated so very far anyhow. I think in my present incarnation the passion that I have for taking Turkish baths may be some slight reaction from my life in the previous and superior conditions as a Tibetan Lama!

The following morning, in cold weather, as usual, we left to try and push our camp as high up as possible. We found a fairly good site, protected to a small extent from the prevailing West wind, and there we collected the whole of our outfit and pitched our camp. I do not think such an enormous cavalcade could possibly have mounted the Rongbuk Glacier before. There were over 300 baggage animals, about twenty ponies, fifty or sixty men in our own employ, and the best part of one hundred Tibetans. Finally, all were paid off, and the Expedition was left alone in its glory. The date was the 1st of May, 1922.

THE FIRST ATTEMPT (WITHOUT OXYGEN)
by George Leigh-Mallory

(Party led by George Leigh-Mallory, accompanied by Major Morshead, Dr Somervell and Major Norton)

A friend of mine once told me he'd caught himself thinking of the Matterhorn with no more reverence than the practised golfer has for an artificial bunker. He believed he should give up climbing mountains until he had recovered his reverence for them. This, I felt, was a commendable attitude in him for it is too easy to present each new ascent as a glorification of man at the expense of the mountains themselves. Mount Everest, apart from its pre-eminence in bulk and height, is great and beautiful, marvellously built, majestic, terrible, a mountain made for reverence: and beneath its shining sides one must stand in awe and wonder.

When we think of a party of climbers struggling along the final ridge of Mount Everest, we are perhaps inclined to reject an obvious comparison of their endeavour with that of athletes in a long distance race. The climbers are not of course competing to reach the goal one before another; the aim is for all to reach it. But the climbers' performance, like the runners', will depend on two factors, endurance and pace. A climber must move at a pace that will allow him, having started from a given point, to reach the top and come down in a given time. It is pace more than anything else which becomes the test of fitness on Mount Everest.

The simpler phenomena of acclimatisation have frequently been referred to in connection with Mount Everest. But still it may be asked why improvement should be expected during a sojourn at 15,000 feet. It is expected because as a matter of experience it happens. Whatever explanation may be given I shall not cease to regard this amazing change as the best of miracles. Even so, if you cut off the supply of fuel you cannot expect your engine to maintain its pace of working; the power exercised by the climber in the more rarefied atmosphere at these high altitudes must be less; a rise of 6,000 feet a day will be beyond his capacity. Therefore he must have camps higher on the mountain, and ultimately he must have one so high that in nine or ten hours even his snail's pace will bring him to the summit. We must remember too that not only will his pace have suffered, his mind will be in a deplorable state. Mountaineers have often observed a lack of clarity in their mental state at high altitudes; it is difficult for the stupid mind to observe how stupid it is. Not only is it difficult to think straight in thin air, it is difficult to retain the desire to do anything at all. The mere weakness of a man's will when he is starved of oxygen is likely to prevent his success. Our continuous process of acclimatisation was due to begin at Phari Dzong. There we should stay three days above 14,000 feet, and after that our marches would keep us between that level and 17,000 feet, so that a man would surely find out how he was affected by living at high altitudes.

After two practice climbs on the way, ten days later we reached our Base Camp at the foot of the Rongbuk Glacier (16,800 feet) and contemplated the prospect of rising another 12,000 feet and more to the summit of Mount Everest. At all events the whole party had reached this point remarkably fit.

In the calculation of what will be required at various stages in order to reach the summit of Mount Everest it is necessary to begin at the highest; and the climber imagines in the first place where he would like to have his camps. He may imagine that on the final day he might rise 2,000 feet to the summit; if he is to give himself the best chance of success he will not wish to start much lower than 27,000 feet, for he is very unlikely to find a place on the ridge above the North-east shoulder (27,400 feet) or on the steep rocks within 200 feet of it. We may therefore fix 27,000 feet approximately as the desirable height for the last camp. And we have another camping ground fixed for us by circumstances, at approximately 23,000 feet, the broad shelf lying in the shelter of the ice-cliffs on the North Col. But to carry up a camp 4,000 feet at these altitudes would be to ask altogether too much of the porters. We must therefore establish an intermediary camp between these two, say at 25,000 feet if a place can be found. Granted then that the best hope is for four men to start from a camp at 27,000 feet, we have firstly to provide them with tents, and they must have sleeping-bags, provisions for two days, fuel and cooking-pots. All these necessities have been previously carried up to the camp below at 25,000 feet; but other things besides are required there. We may assume that this camp is to be used as a stage on the way up only and not on the way down. Even so, six porters at least will have to sleep there before carrying up the highest camp, and their requirements will be the same as we have laid down for the four climbers. It will be understood from this method of calculation how we arrive at the number of loads which must be carried up to any given camp.

With the prospect of an early monsoon, on 10 May Somervell and I started from the Base Camp for Camp I. We found that an adequate path had already been stamped on the loose moraine, so that we could walk comfortably from one camp to the other in two hours and a half. Moreover we were highly pleased by Camp I. Geoffrey Bruce had been busy here with certain constructional works. We found a little house reserved for Europeans, one of four solidly built with stones and roofed with the outer flies of Whymper tents. The greater part of our alpine stores, with which I was especially concerned, had already reached Camp I. Next morning, having sorted our stores, we started for Camp II.

We mildly followed where the route had been laid out by Colonel Strutt and his party and found the glacier far less broken than was to be expected. We descended it abruptly, to find ourselves on the flat space where Camp II was situated. Beyond and above us was a vast mountain of reddish rock known to us only by the triangulated height of its sharp summit, marked in Wheeler's map as 23,180. The pinnacles became more thickly crowded together as we mounted, until, as we followed the bend southwards, individuals were lost in the crowd and finally the crowd was merged into the great tumbled sea of the glacier, now no longer dark with stones, but exhibiting everywhere the bright surfaces of its steep and angry waves. At Camp II we were surrounded on three sides by this amazing world of ice. Nothing, of course, was to be seen of Mount Everest; the whole bulk of the North Peak stood in front of it. Next morning, 12 May, according to Colonel Strutt's directions, we worked our way along the true left edge of the glacier and the stones of its left bank. The reconnaissance party had reached a better surface by only a short and simple crossing of the rougher ice. We easily found the place, marked by a conspicuous cairn, where they had turned away from the bank. Presently we found another cairn built upon a single large stone, and here proceeded with confidence to cross a deep and wide trough of which we had been warned; and once this obstacle was overcome we knew no difficulty could impede our progress to Camp III. The laden porters, however, did not get along very easily, so we decided to supply them with crampons, which they subsequently found very useful on this stage of the journey.

The situation of Camp III when we reached it early in the afternoon of 12 May was not calculated to encourage me. Here we should have the sun early, but we should lose it early too, and we observed with dismay on this first afternoon that our camp was in shadow at 3.15 p.m. The water supply was conveniently near, running in a trough, and we might expect it to be unfrozen for several hours each day. Very little energy remained among the party, most of whom had now reached 21,000 feet for the first time in their lives. After ground for the two tents was levelled, we sent down the main body of the porters, keeping only one man for cook and each the man specially attached to him as servant by Bruce's command long ago in Darjeeling.

It was our intention on the following morning, 13 May, to take with us two available porters and so make a small beginning towards the supply of our next camp. But Somervell's man was sick. We set out in good time with only my porter, Dasno. With the sun behind us we saw the first long slope, nearly 1,000 feet, glittering in a way that snow will never glitter; there we should find only blue ice, bare and hard. The more we thought about it the more convinced we became that an alternative way must be found up to this final slope. Unless the connection between Camps III and IV were free from serious obstacles, the whole problem of transport would increase enormously in difficulty. We soon determined that we should make use of a sloping corridor lying some distance to the left of the icy line used last year and apparently covered with snow. Here fortune favoured our enterprise. In the disintegrated substance of its edges it was hardly necessary to cut steps,

and we mounted 250 feet of what threatened to be formidable ice with no great expenditure of time and energy. Two lengths of rope were now fixed for the security of future parties. Past the foot of the North-west ridge we looked down the immense glacier flowing South-westwards into Nepal. We were enchanted by the spectacle of Pumori; though its summit (23,190 feet) was little higher than our own level, it was, as it always is, a singularly impressive sight. The snow-cap of Pumori is supported by splendid architecture; the pyramidal bulk of the mountain, the steep fall of the ridges and faces to South and West, and the precipices of rock and ice towards East and North, are set off by a whole chain of mountains extending West-north-west along a frail, fantastic ridge unrivalled anywhere in this district for the elegant beauty of its cornices and towers.

We sped again over snow-covered monticules thrust up from the chaos of riven ice, and at last looked down from one more prominent little summit to the very nape of the Chang La. We saw our conjectured shelf in real existence and a fair way before us. In a moment all our doubts were eased. We knew that the foot of the North Ridge, by which alone we could approach the summit of Mount Everest, was not beyond our reach.

It was four o'clock. The tent which Dasno had carried up was left to be the symbol of our future intentions, and we hastened down. Since 7 a.m. Somervell and I had been spending our strength with only one considerable halt, and latterly at a rapid rate. For some hours now we had felt the dull height-headache which results from exertion with too little oxygen, a symptom, I am told, not unlike the effect of poisoning by carbon monoxide. I was very glad to reach our tent again at Camp III. I took a little soup and could face no food; defeated for the first and last time in either expedition before the sight of supper. I humbly swallowed a dose of aspirin, lay my head on the pillow and went to sleep. In a sleeping-bag such as we had this year, with soft flannel lining the quilted eiderdown, one need not be chilled even by the coldest night; and to lie in a tent no bigger than will just hold two persons, with twenty degrees of frost inside and forty degrees without, snugly defying cold and wind, to experience at once this situation, the keen bite of the air and the warm glow in one's extremities, gives a delicious sensation of well-being and true comfort never to be so acutely provoked even in the armchair at an English fireside.

On 16 May Somervell and I spent the morning in camp with some hopes of welcoming sooner or later the arrival of stores, and sure enough about midday the first detachment of a large convoy reached our camp. With the porters, somewhat to our surprise, were Strutt, Morshead and Norton. It had hitherto been assumed that the first attempt should be made only by Somervell and I, and General Bruce had not cancelled our orders. Strutt saw no reason why the four of us should be too many for one party provided our organisation sufficed. Norton and Morshead were evidently most anxious to come and for my part I had always held, and still held, the view that four climbers were a sounder party than two for this sort of mountaineering.

To carry the whole of what we should need up to Camp IV in one journey was clearly impossible. But we reckoned that twenty loads should be enough to provide for ourselves and for nine porters, who would have to sleep there and carry up another camp. The delay in making two journeys to the North Col was not too great. On 17 May the fifteen of us, Strutt, Morshead, Norton, Somervell and I, with ten porters, set off for Camp IV. On 19 May we carried up the remainder of our loads, and we seemed better acclimatised. The ascent to the North Col was generally felt to be easier on this day. With all our loads now gathered about us at Camp IV the first stage up from the base of the mountain was accomplished.

With our aluminium cooking sets we could use either absolute alcohol in the spirit-burner or 'Meta', a French sort of solidified spirit, especially prepared in cylindrical shape and extremely efficient; it burns without any trouble, and smokelessly, even at 23,000 feet, for not less than forty minutes. So good was the tea we made that I came almost to disregard the objectionable flavour of tinned milk in it. The two liquid foods, cocoa and pea-soup, though not imbibed so plentifully as tea, were considered no less as the natural and fitting companions on any and every occasion – 'The foundation of every dish must be pea-soup' – it was a corollary of this axiom that any and every available solid food might be used to stew with pea-soup. It was this that we ate at Camp IV, about the hour of an early afternoon tea on 19 May: here were the four of us fit and happy, to all appearances as we should expect to be in a snug alpine hut after a proper nightcap of whisky punch!

My first recollection of the morning of 20 May is of shivering outside the porters' tents. It is not an enviable task at 23,000 feet, this of rousing men from the snugness of their sleeping-bags between 5 and 6 a.m. Of our nine porters it was presently discovered that five were mountain-sick in various degrees; only four were fit to come on and do a full day's work carrying up our camp. Morshead, who seemed the fittest of us all, was set to lead the party. I followed with two porters, while Norton and Somervell shepherded the others on a separate rope. We presently found the stones agreeably secure; enough snow lay among them to bind and freeze all to the slope; no sort of ground could have taken us more easily up the mountain. The morning, too, was calm and fine, but the air remained perceptibly colder than we could have wished. For my part, I added a light shetland 'woolly' and a thin silk shirt to what I was wearing before under my closely woven cotton coat. As this outer garment, with knickers to match, was practically windproof, and a silk shirt too is a further protection against wind, with these two extra layers I feared no cold we were likely to meet.

At one point Norton was sitting a little way below with his rucksack poised on his lap. Its balance was upset, he was unprepared, made a desperate grab, and missed it. Slowly the round, soft thing gathered momentum from its rotation, the first little leaps down from one ledge to another grew to excited and magnificent bounds, and the precious burden vanished from sight.

I cannot say precisely how much time passed on this arduous section of our ascent. It was now 11.30 a.m. The aneroid was showing 25,000 feet; the rise of 2,000 feet had taken us in all 3½ hours. It was 12.30 p.m. before the stragglers who had joined us had rested sufficiently to go on. To fix a camp 1,000 feet higher would probably require, granted reasonably good fortune in finding a site, another three hours. At about 2 p.m. Somervell and some porter shouted the news that one tent could be pitched in the place where they were. It remained to find a place near at hand for the other tent. We chose the foot of a long sloping slab – at all events it was part of the mountain and would not budge. Our tent was pitched at last with one side of the floor lying along the foot of the sloping slab and the other half on the platform we had made. Before we had concluded these operations the porters had been sent down at about 3 p.m., a kitchen had been instituted, and a meal was already being prepared.

The two small tents stood perched there on the vast mountain-side of snow-bound rocks and actually higher, at 25,000 feet, than any climbing party had been before. 'Hang it all!' we cooed, 'it's not so bad.' In the early morning we were listening to the musical patter of fine, granular snow on the roofs of our tents. A second rucksack escaped us, slipping from the ledge where it was perched, and went bounding down the mountain. It contained our provisions; our breakfast was inside it. Somehow or another it was hung up on a ledge 100 feet below. Morshead volunteered to go and get it. By slow degrees he dragged the heavy load, and our precious stores were recovered intact.

At 8 a.m. we were ready to start and roped up, Norton first, followed by myself, Morshead and

Mallory and Norton approaching their highest point

Somervell. We had only moved upwards a few steps when Morshead stopped. 'I think I won't come with you any further,' he said. 'I know I should only keep you back.' It was decided he should remain in camp while we three went on without him.

Our first object was to regain the crest of the North ridge, by slanting up to meet it perhaps 800 feet above us. We wanted to hit off just that mean pace which we could keep up without rapidly losing our strength, and with the occasional help of the hands we were able to keep going for spells of twenty or thirty minutes before halting for three, four or five minutes.

It was our intention naturally in setting out this day to reach the summit of Mount Everest. From the outset we were short of time; we should have started two hours earlier but the weather prevented us. The fresh snow was an encumbrance, lying everywhere on the ledges from four to eight inches deep; when we measured our rate of progress it was not satisfactory, at most 400 feet an hour. It became clear we should still, at the best, be struggling upwards after night had fallen again. We were prepared to leave it to braver men to climb Mount Everest by night. By agreeing to this arithmetical computation we tacitly accepted defeat. We were not greatly interested then in the exact number of feet by which we should beat a record.

Looking back on my own mental processes as we approached 27,000 feet, I can find nothing completely illogical; within a small compass I was able to reason. But my reasoning was concerned only with one idea. The view for instance, did not interest me, I had not even the desire to look over the North-east ridge; I had no strong desire to get there, and none at all for the wonder of being there. It seemed to me that we should get back to Morshead in time to take him down this same day to Camp IV. The idea of reaching Camp IV with Morshead before dark, once it had been accepted, controlled us altogether. At 2.15 we completed the ascent of a steeper pitch and

found ourselves on the edge of an easier terrain, where the mountain slopes back towards the North-east shoulder. It was an obvious place for a halt. Our aneroid was reading 26,800; we were glad to have the confirmation of the theodolite later, proving that we had reached 26,985 feet.

We had no chance of finding water here and medical opinion, which knew all about what was good for us, frowned upon the notion of alcoholic stimulant for a climber in distress at a high altitude. And so, very naturally, when one of us produced from his pocket a flask of brandy – each of us took a little nip. I am glad to relate the result was excellent; it is logically certain therefore that the brandy contained no alcohol!

I announced that I would take the lead. Norton and I changed places on the rope. We were obliged to work back to the ridge itself and follow it down in our morning's tracks. At 4 p.m. we reached our camp, where Morshead was waiting. We had now to descend only 2,000 feet to Camp IV, and with more than three hours' daylight left we supposed we should have no difficulty in reaching our tents before dark.

But though the party was a stage nearer to the end of the journey, it was also a stage nearer to exhaustion and to that state where carelessness so readily slips in unperceived. The fresh snow fallen during the night had so altered appearances that we could not be certain that we were exactly following the line by which we had approached our camp the day before. My impression is that we went too low and missed it. It was not a difficult place and yet not easy, just the sort to catch a tired party off their guard.

The whole party would not necessarily have been in grave danger had not one man lost his footing. But we were unprepared. When the third man slipped the last man was moving, and was at once pulled off his balance. The second in the party, though he must have checked these two, could not hold them. In a moment the three of them were slipping down and gathering speed on a slope where nothing would stop them until they reached the plateau of the East Rong-buk Glacier, 3,500 feet below. The leader, though he could see nothing of what went on behind him, was on the alert; warned now by unusual sounds that something was wrong, he at once struck the pick of his axe into the snow, and hitched the rope round the head of it. The rope suddenly tightened and tugged at the axe-head. It gave a little as it gripped the metal like a hawser on a bollard. The pick did not budge. Then the rope came taut between the moving figures, and the rope showed what it was worth. The danger had passed. The weight of three men had not come upon the rope with a single jerk. We were soon secure again on the mountain-side, and – not the least surprising fact – no one had been hurt.

When we reached the ridge and again looked down at the snow where we had come up the day before, though it was clear enough we must waste no time, we did not feel greatly pressed. We had still an hour of daylight. I had been aware for some time that Morshead, though he was going steadily and well, was more tired than the rest of us, and at best he could move downwards a few steps at a time. So we crawled down the mountain-side in the gathering darkness, and were still stumbling on in the dark without a lantern when we reached the North Col. Two hundred yards, or a little more in a direct line, now separated us from our tents, with the promise of safety, repose, and warmth in our soft eiderdown bags. But the tracks were concealed, and not to be found; crevasses lay under the snow waiting for us.

We had only to find the rope which had been fixed on the steep slope below us and we should be at the end of our troubles. But the rope was deeply buried, and we searched in vain, dragging the snow with our picks along the edge of the fall. We were still searching when the last of our candle burnt out. In the end we must do without the rope, and began the abrupt

Captain Noel kinematographing the ascent of Mount Everest with his high power telescopic camera

descent tentatively, dubiously, uncertain that we had hit off the right place. The situation was decidedly disagreeable. Suddenly someone among us hitched up the rope from under the snow. Then, at 11.30 p.m. we fumbled at the tent-doors, at last we began to say 'Thank God.'

We must melt snow and have water. But where were the cooking-pots? We searched the tents without finding a trace of them. Presumably the porters had taken them down to Camp III in error. Still supperless, we wriggled into our sleeping-bags. Then Norton had an idea; we had the means at hand to make ice-creams he said. A tin of strawberry jam was opened; frozen Ideal Milk was hacked out of another; these two ingredients were mixed with snow, and it only remained to eat the compound. The last stage of our descent to Camp III had still to be accomplished on the following morning of 22 May. I imagine that a fresh man with old tracks to help him might cover the distance from Camp IV in about an hour and a quarter. But no sign was left of our old tracks, and the snow was deeper here than higher up. The wearisome descent, which began at 6 a.m., continued far into the morning.

Reinforcements had arrived at Camp III in our absence, and the transport had worked with such wonderful speed that the oxygen cylinders were already in action. Finch, whom we had last heard of in bed with dysentery at the Base Camp, had shown such energy that he was now testing the oxygen apparatus with Wakefield and Geoffrey Bruce. Wakefield now took us in charge, and at noon we were at Camp III once more. Strutt and Morris had come out to meet us. Noel had stayed in camp, and, like a tormentor waiting for his disarmed victim, there we found the 'movie' camera and him winding the handle.

However, our welcome in camp is a pleasing memory. The supply of tea was inexhaustible. Somervell confesses to have drunk seventeen mugfuls; he can hardly have been so moderate.

THE SECOND ATTEMPT (WITH OXYGEN)
by Captain George Finch

(Party led by Captain George Finch, accompanied by Brigadier General Geoffrey Bruce and Lance-Corporal Tejbir)

With the departure of the last of our companions on 27 March, Crawford and I found ourselves left behind in Darjeeling impatiently awaiting the arrival of the oxygen equipment from Calcutta. We ultimately rejoined the main body of the Expedition in Kampa Dzong on 13 April. Our journey towards the Base Camp led us towards the West across Tibet.

Like all humankind the Tibetans have their bad as well as their good points. The former are easily told. If one wishes to converse with a Tibetan, it is always advisable to stand on his windward side. A noble Tibetan once boasted that during his lifetime he had had two baths – one on the occasion of his birth, the other on the day of his marriage. Those of us honoured by his presence found the statement difficult to believe. Apart from this rather penetrating drawback, the Tibetans are a most likeable people; cheery, contented, good-natured, and hard-working; slow to give a promise, but punctilious to a degree in carrying it out; truthful and scrupulously honest.

The priests, or 'Lamas' as they are called in Tibet, constitute the governing class. The monasteries are the seats of learning. I regret to state that I did not like the priests as much as the laity. The reason is not far to seek. If you wish to hold converse with a Lama, it is advisable not only to stand on his windward side, but also to take care that the wind is exceptionally strong, it will be readily understood that the odour of sanctity is all-pervading. In other respects the monks proved as attractive as their simpler countrymen.

Kindly, courteous, and appreciative of little attentions, they were always ready to lend assistance and to give information concerning their religion and the manners and customs of their country. These few of

Karma Paul, the expedition's interpreter

Romoo, the Lepcha collector

the more lasting of my impressions would be incomplete without mention of Tibetan music. In point of view of sheer ugliness of sound, it competes with the jarring, clashing squeaks, bangs, and hoots of the jazz-bands that were so fashionable at home at the time of our departure for India.

On 2 May, the day after our arrival at the Base Camp, frequent oxygen drills were held, and all the oxygen stores overhauled and tested. On consulting my diary, I find that during the period from 1 May to 5 June, there were two days when the weather was fine and settled, and that these two days succeeded snowstorms which had thickly powdered the mountain with fresh snow.

On 10 May, Mallory and Somervell set out for Camp III, to make ready for a first attempt to climb Mount Everest. On 15 May, I was ready and eager to think about doing something. My climbing compan-

The camp at the north east shoulder of Mount Everest

ions were Geoffrey Bruce and Lance-Corporal Tejbir, the most promising of the Ghurkas.

Leaving the Base on the 16th we proceeded to Camp I, where the following day was spent attending to our oxygen apparatus and transport arrangements. Soon after midday on the 18th, we arrived at Camp II. On the 19th we reached Camp III, where we learned from Colonel Strutt that Mallory, Norton, Somervell, and Morshead had gone up to the North Col in the morning.

The cylinders containing our oxygen were found to be in good condition; but the apparatus – through no fault of the makers, who had, indeed, done their work admirably – leaked very badly, and to get them into satisfactory working order, four days of hard toil with soldering-iron, hacksaw and pliers were necessary. Preparatory to embarking on the climb itself, we went for several trial walks – one over to the Rapiu La, a pass 21,000 feet high. Colonel Strutt and Dr Wakefield, unoxygenated, accompanied us on this little expedition, and oxygen at once proved its value, so easily did Bruce and I outpace them. On 22 May, acting on instructions from Colonel Strutt, Geoffrey Bruce, Wakefield, Tejbir and I, with a number of porters, set out for the North Col to meet and afford any required assistance to the members of the first climbing party who were on their way down from the mountain. We met them just above the foot of the final steep slopes leading up to the North Col. They were more or less in the last stage of exhaustion, as, indeed, men who have done their best on such a mountain should be.

On 24 May, Captain Noel, Tejbir, Geoffrey Bruce and I, all using oxygen, went up to the North Col (23,000 feet). Bent on a determined attack, we camped there for the night. Morning broke fine and clear though somewhat windy, and at eight o'clock we set off up the long snow-slopes leading towards the North-east shoulder of Mount Everest, twelve porters carrying oxygen cylinders, provisions for one day, and camping gear. An hour and a half later, Bruce,

Tejbir and I followed, and, in spite of the fact that each bore a load of over 30 lb, which was much more than the average weight carried by the porters, we overtook them at a height of about 24,500 feet. They greeted our arrival with their usual cheery, broad grins. The porters at least appreciated the advantages of what they naively chose to call 'English air'. Shortly after one o'clock the wind freshened up rather offensively, and it began to snow. Our altitude was

The oxygen apparatus in use

25,500 feet, some 500 feet below where we had hoped to camp. The porters arrived at 2 p.m., and at once all began to level off the little platform where the tent was soon pitched, on the very edge of the tremendous precipices falling away to the East Rongbuk and Main Rongbuk Glaciers, over 4,000 feet below. Within twenty minutes the porters were scurrying back down the broken, rocky ridge towards the snow-slopes.

I joined Bruce and Tejbir inside the tent. It was snowing hard. After sunset, the storm rose to a gale. Sleep was out of the question. We dared not relax our vigilance, for all our strength was needed to hold the tent down. By one o'clock on the morning of the 26th the gale reached its maximum. Dawn broke bleak and chill; the snow had ceased to fall, but the wind continued with unabated violence. At noon the storm once more regained its strength and rose to unsurpassed fury. But I wanted to hang on and try our climb on the following day. Bruce jumped at the idea, and when our plans were communicated to Tejbir, the only effect upon him was to broaden his already expansive grin. We connected up the apparatus in such a way that we could breathe a small quantity of oxygen throughout the night. The result was marvellous. We slept well and warmly. There is little doubt that it was the use of oxygen which saved our lives during this second night in our high camp.

Before daybreak we were up, but putting on our boots was a struggle, Bruce's and Tejbir's were frozen solid, and it took them more than an hour to mould them into shape by holding them over lighted candles. At 6.30 a.m. we shouldered our bundles and set off. What with cameras, thermos bottles, and oxygen apparatus, Bruce and I each carried well over forty pounds; Tejbir with two extra cylinders of oxygen shouldered a burden of about fifty pounds. Our scheme of attack was to take Tejbir with us as far as the North-east shoulder, there to relieve him of his load and send him back. The weather was clear, but it soon freshened and the cold began to have its effect on Tejbir's sturdy constitution. At 26,000 feet he collapsed entirely, sinking face downwards on to the rocks and crushing beneath him the delicate instruments of his oxygen apparatus. We pulled him off his apparatus and, relieving him of some cylinders, cheered him up sufficiently to start him with enough oxygen on his way back to the high camp there to await our return.

Climbing quite easy rocks we gained an altitude of 26,500 feet. By this time, however, the wind, which had been steadily rising, had acquired such force that I considered it necessary to leave the ridge and continue our ascent by traversing out across the great northern face of Mount Everest, hoping by so doing to find more shelter from the icy blasts. Very occasionally in the midst of our exacting work we were forced to indulge in a brief rest in order to replace an empty cylinder of oxygen by a full one. The empty ones were thrown away, and as each bumped its way over the precipice and the good steel clanged like a church bell at each impact, we laughed aloud at the thought that 'There goes another five pounds off our backs'.

Now and then we consulted the aneroid barometer, and its readings encouraged us on. 27,000 feet; then we gave up traversing and began to climb diagonally upwards towards a point on the lofty North-east ridge, midway between the shoulder and the summit. Soon afterwards an accident put Bruce's oxygen apparatus out of action. After connecting him on to my apparatus and so renewing his supply of oxygen, we soon traced the trouble and effected a satisfactory repair. The barometer here recorded a height of 27,300 feet.

Though 1,700 feet below, we were well within half a mile of the summit, so close, indeed, that we could distinguish individual stones on a little patch of scree lying just underneath the highest point. Ours were truly the tortures of Tantalus; for weak from hunger and exhausted by that nightmare struggle for life in our high camp, we were in no fit condition to pro-

The party ascending the higher slopes

*The second climbing party descending
from their record climb*

ceed. Indeed, I knew that if we were to persist in climbing on, even if only for another 500 feet, we should not both get back alive. The decision to retreat once taken, no time was lost, and, fearing lest another accidental interruption in the oxygen supply might lead to a slip on the part of either of us, we roped together. It was midday. Shortly after 2 p.m., we struck the ridge and there reduced our burdens to a minimum by dumping four oxygen cylinders.

The clear weather was gone. We plunged down the easy, broken rocks through thick mists driven past us from the West by a violent wind. We reached our high camp in barely half an hour, and such are the vagaries of Everest's moods that in this short time the wind had practically dropped. Tejbir lay snugly wrapped up in all three sleeping-bags, sleeping the deep sleep of exhaustion. Hearing the voices of the porters on their way up to bring down our kit, we woke him up, telling him to await their arrival and to go down with them. We were deplorably tired, and could no longer move ahead with our accustomed vigour, but eventually we reached the broken snows of the North Col, and arrived in camp there at 4 p.m. Hot tea and a tin of spaghetti were soon forthcoming, and even this little nourishment refreshed us and renewed our strength to such an extent that three-quarters of an hour later we were ready to set off for Camp III. An invaluable addition to our little party was Captain Noel, the indefatigable photographer of the Expedition. He formed our rearguard and nursed us safely down the steep snow and ice slopes on to the almost level basin of the glacier below. Before 5.30 p.m., only forty minutes after leaving the col, we reached Camp III. Since midday, from our highest point we had descended over 6,000 feet; but we were quite finished. Our attack on Mount Everest had failed. The great mountain with its formidable array of defensive weapons had won.

Geoffrey Bruce and I arrived back at the Base Camp early in the afternoon of 29 May. The next few days were spent in resting. However, as the weather appeared fine, and there seemed promise of a bright spell prior to the breaking of the monsoon, it was decided to make another attempt on the mountain. Of the remaining climbing members of the Expedition, Somervell was undoubtedly the fittest, with Mallory a good second. Both had enjoyed some ten days' rest since their first assault upon Mount Everest, and therefore had a chance of recovering from the abnormal strain to which they had been submitted.

On 3 June we left the Base Camp. The party consisted of Wakefield as M.O., Crawford, and later Morris, as transport officers, Mallory, Somervell and myself as climbers. The attempt was to be made with oxygen, and I was placed in command. It required a great effort for me to get as far as Camp I, and I realised there that the few days' rest which I had enjoyed at the Base Camp had been quite insufficient to allow my recuperation. After giving Somervell final detailed instructions regarding the oxygen apparatus, I wished them all the best of luck, and on the 4th returned to the Base Camp. As Strutt, Longstaff, and Morshead were leaving next day for Darjeeling, I was given, and availed myself of, the opportunity of accompanying them.

THE THIRD ATTEMPT (WITH OXYGEN)
by George Leigh-Mallory

(Party led by George Leigh-Mallory accompanied by Dr Somervell)

The project of making a third attempt this season was mooted immediately on the return of Finch and Geoffrey Bruce to the Base Camp. The difficulty was to find a party. Of the six who had been already engaged only one was obviously fit for another great effort. Somervell had shown a recuperative capacity beyond the rest of us and Finch was not yet to be counted out. We at once arranged that Somervell, Finch and I, together with Wakefield and Crawford, should set

forth the same day. The monsoon was usually to be expected about 10 June, and we knew that it was late last year, the signs of its approach were gathering every day.

The signs were even more ominous than usual as Finch and I walked up to Camp I on the afternoon of 3 June. We had not long disposed ourselves comfortably within four square walls of our 'sangar', when snow began to fall. Released at last by the West wind which had held it back, the monsoon was free to work its will, and we soon understood that the great change of weather had now come.

Finch wisely decided to go back, and we charged him with a message to General Bruce, saying that we saw no reason at present to alter our plans. It was not unreasonable to expect an interval of fine weather after the first heavy snow, and with eight or ten fair days a third attempt might still be made. After a second night of unremitting snowfall the weather on the morning of 5 June improved and we decided to go on. We passed Camp II, not requiring to halt at this stage, and were well up towards Camp III before the fresh snow became a serious impediment.

The tents at Camp III had been struck for the safety of the poles, but not packed up. The stores were all buried; everything that we wanted had first to be dug out. But the next morning broke fine; we had soon a clear sky and glorious sunshine; it was the warmest day that any of us remembered at Camp III. We had already resolved to use oxygen on the third attempt. Somervell, after Finch's explanation of the mechanical details, felt perfectly confident that he could manage the oxygen apparatus. But whereas they had started using it at 21,000 feet, we intended to go up to our old camp at 25,000 feet without it, perhaps use a cylinder each up to 26,000 feet, and at all events start from that height for the summit with a full supply of four cylinders.

The party, Somervell, Crawford and I, with fourteen porters (Wakefield was to be supply officer at Camp III), set out at 8 a.m. At 10.15 a.m., Somervell,

I, a porter, and Crawford roped up in that order, began to work up the steep ice-slope, now covered with snow. It was clear that the three of us without loads must take the lead in turns stamping out the track for our porters. No trace was found of our previous tracks, and we were soon arguing as to where exactly they might be as we slanted across the slope. Everything was done by trenching the snow to induce it to come down if it would; every test gave a satisfactory result. If the snow would not come down where we had formerly encountered steep bare ice, *a fortiori*, above, on the gentler slopes, we had nothing to fear. The thought of an avalanche was dismissed from our minds.

About 1.30 p.m. I halted and the porters, following on three separate ropes, soon came up with the leading party. We were now about 400 feet below a conspicuous block of ice and 600 feet below Camp IV, still on the gentle slopes of the corridor. We were startled by an ominous sound, sharp, arresting, violent, and yet somehow soft like an explosion of untamped gunpowder. In a moment I observed the surface of the snow broken and puckered where it had been even for a few yards to the right of me. And then I began to move slowly downwards, inevitably carried on the whole moving surface by a force I was utterly powerless to resist.

For a second or two I seemed hardly to be in danger as I went quietly sliding down with the snow. Then the rope at my waist tightened and held me back. A wave of snow came over me and I was buried. I thrust out my arms above my head and actually went through some sort of motions of swimming on my back. I felt an increasing pressure about my body. I wondered how tightly I should be squeezed and then the avalanche came to rest. My arms were free; my legs were near the surface. After a brief struggle, I was standing again, surprised and breathless, in the motionless snow. But the rope was tight at my waist: the porter tied on next to me, I supposed, must be deeply buried. To my further

surprise he quickly emerged unharmed as myself. Somervell and Crawford too, though they had been above me by the rope's length, were now quite close, and soon extricated themselves.

Looking down over the foam of snow, we saw one group of porters at some little distance, perhaps 150 feet below us. Presumably the others must be buried somewhere between us and them. We soon made out that they were the party who had been immediately behind us, and they were pointing below them. The other two parties, one of four and one of five men roped together, must have been carried even further. But as we hurried down we soon saw that beneath the place where the four porters were standing was a formidable drop; it was only too plain that the missing men had been swept over it. We had no difficulty in finding a way round this obstacle. Our fears were soon confirmed. One man was quickly uncovered and found to be still breathing; before long we were certain that he would live. Another whom we dug out near him had been killed by the fall. A loop of rope which we pulled up convinced us that the other party must be here, and we were able to follow the rope to the bodies. One was dug up lifeless; another was found upside down, and when we uncovered his face Somervell thought he was still breathing. We had the greatest difficulty in extricating this man, so tightly was the snow packed about his limbs; his load, four oxygen cylinders on a steel frame, had to be cut from his back.

Though buried for about forty minutes, he had survived the fall and the suffocation, and suffered no serious harm. Of the two others in this party of four, we found only one. Of the other five, all the bodies were recovered, but only one was alive. The two who had so marvellously escaped were able to walk down to Camp III, and were almost perfectly well next day. The other seven were killed.

This tragic calamity was naturally the end of the third attempt to climb Mount Everest. We asked the porters whether they wished to go up and bring down

A frost-bitten climber being helped down to Camp Two

the bodies for orderly burial. They preferred to leave them where they were. In their honour a large cairn was built at Camp III.

The Expedition had failed in its purpose to conquer Everest, but valuable experience had been gained for a future attempt. There can be no doubt about one point; the final camp was too low at 25,000 feet. Another point upon which we were all agreed was that it was not so much the normal exertion of climbing that was unduly exhausting, but the addition of anything that was unexpected, such as cutting steps, or having to raise the pace of the ascent. The value of oxygen for restoring exhausted men was sufficiently well illustrated during our second attempt, but, for my part, I don't think it impossible to get up without oxygen. However, if the weight of the oxygen equipment could be reduced by fifty per cent, it would alter the whole nature of the problem.

It is hoped that our successes as well as our failures will be a guide to any future attempt, but one thing remains true; Everest will never be climbed without men who have the determination to carry through the high project, and the simple will to conquer in the struggle.

Pearls and Savages

Like Marco Polo, Frank Hurley was 'moved by a great curiosity'. It is unquenchable wonder that motivated the travels and pervades the writings of this remarkable traveller. Yet traveller is not the right word — adventurer is, or explorer. Traveller is too light; it may serve to describe the Thesigers and Shackletons of today with their sophisticated aids to success and survival, but it won't do for someone of the calibre of Hurley who displayed from the beginning to the end of his long professional career, the 'most essential qualities of all explorers — initiative and curiosity'. By the time he had published *Pearls and Savages* in 1924, Hurley had already completed three epic journeys including in 1911–12 to the South Magnetic Pole with Douglas Mawson.

Pearls and Savages is the account of Hurley's journey into the interior of unexplored New Guinea to meet the fabled head-hunters and cannibals and 'men of the Stone Age'. He took with him one light-draught vessel; the *Eureka*, one seaplane, the *Seagull*, eight natives from Port Moresby and four whites from Australia: McCulloch, the Natural Historian; Lang, the pilot; Hill, the engineer; and Bell, the navigator. They spent eight months in the interior, navigating their dangerous and depressing, enlightening and exhilarating way up the Fly River to the daunting, haunting shores of Lake Murray, meeting and coming to some elementary human terms with the 'men from the Stone Age' who believed that the White Man's shaving soap was the way he kept the colour of his skin.

Hurley's account of the journey is straightforward and unflamboyant. On the few occasions he allows his eloquence to emerge, it is to transmit his wonder at the beauty of nature. And on the few occasions he allows his philosophy to peep through, it is shy as if, here too, he was entering unsure country. Perhaps, like wonder, humility was the mark of the early explorer. Hurley's true gift, in fact, was the picture not the prose. In limiting Hurley to some of his prose and a few of his pictures, the hope is that the essence of the man will come through — the initiative that made him a true explorer, and the wonder that made him a true adventurer.

Portrait of Frank Hurley filming in Antarctica. Here his ship was caught in the ice and crushed

Frank Hurley filming in Papua, New Guinea

VOYAGES IN THE AIR, ON LAND AND SEA IN NEW GUINEA, 1924, by Captain Frank Hurley

A FORGOTTEN LAND OUT OF THE STONE AGE: PAPUA AND THE TORRES STRAITS

Cape York, the northernmost limit of the island continent Australia, frays out into an archipelago of islets which litter the Torres Straits and extend across to the shores of New Guinea one hundred miles to the north. Spanish and Portuguese voyagers in search of treasure lands passed this way only to meet a doom upon the reefs, unrecorded save for copper fragments and corroded coins brought to the eyes of a wondering world by the pearl divers. What became of the crews of the vessels? Were they butchered by the bloodthirsty hordes or were they permitted to mingle with the tribe and so indelibly stamp certain featural characteristics upon the present generations? Could this account for the marked Spanish and Hebraic types that today inhabit the regions contiguous to the reefs?

The northern boundary of Torres Straits is like the threshold of Despair. This strange land is one of the world's last regions of mystery – some 90,000 square miles. Beyond the coastal littoral lies the *terra incognita* inhabited by savages as lawless and primitive as they were at the dawn of creation.

The rugged and impenetrable nature of the country renders the work of exploration laborious and tardy, and the process of establishing friendly relations with cannibals and head-hunters by moral suasion, strings of beads and iron axes, needs daring, resource and disregard for such trite receptions as showers of arrows and stone clubs. Occasionally an inquisitive wanderer in uncontrolled areas loses his head, but as it is reverentially preserved in the tribal Valhalla with other similar trophies, there is some consolation and posthumous glory in an original demise which suddenly transforms one from a nonentity in life to a famous martyr in death.

The people themselves are a puzzle, rarely moving in their primitive state beyond the purlieus of their own villages for fear of hostile neighbours; indulging still in the most barbaric rites and fantastic ceremonies, and as diverse in type and physique as the endless dialects they speak. Behind the vast and shallow expanse of the Gulf of Papua the most interesting and pristine division is to be found. Here the people are mostly head-hunters and cannibals, characterized by a rich ceremonial life, and indulging still in a form of ancestor worship and skull-cult. The modes of dress vary with the tribes – shells, grass sporrans, fibre skirts, and chic creations and beaten-out bark which leave alike much to the imagination and to the mosquitoes.

New Guinea – there is more glory and beauty in this enchanted land than I dreamed this world contained. The brand of commerce has scarcely touched these shores. The slayer of the forest has not even disturbed the birds. The land is as nature made it.

HEAD-HUNTING STATESMEN AND DIPLOMATS: COIR, THE LORD MAYOR, AND GORMIER, MINISTER OF WAR AT URAMA

Travelling by water from the inland swamps fed by the drainage from the Owen Stanley ranges we reached the junction of the Aramia and the mighty Bamu rivers and drew into the sheltered waters of Kerewa behind the Island of Goaribari.

The Goaribaries are conspicuous by the amount of ornate trappings which they wear. No Goaribari is dressed without his leggings which fit the calf tightly and are adorned up the front by two rows of small cowrie shells. The women load their arms with the highly valued armlet shells and adorn the breasts with shapely crescents cut from the mother-o'-pearl shell. They wear many-rowed necklaces of beads and band their shaven crowns in a manner that must be a sore encumbrance. The men are of medium build, well

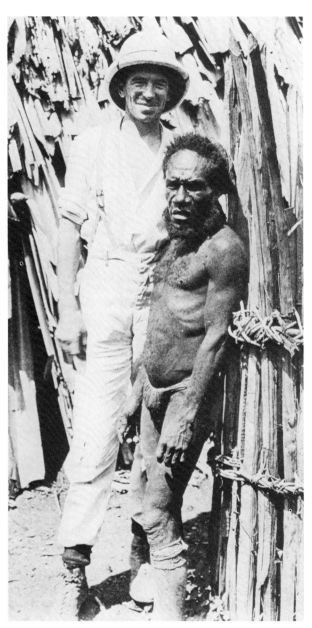

Frank Hurley with one of the chiefs he met

proportioned, and look as though food were abundant. Of the women a few might be regarded as comely – but a very few. Apart from a grass belt and a very narrow strip of fibre – they are unclothed. The men wear more: a large cumbersome section cut from the bailer shell, a very ornate belt of carved bark and a strange bundle of teased fibre or grass that falls behind like a bushy tail conveying the impression of a richly caparisoned draught horse.

The long house extends along the river bank for no less than 500 feet, constructed from lashed mangrove saplings and thatched with the leaf of the sago palm. It stands some five feet off the ground on a jungle of piles.

The first objects that attracted our attention were small groups of skulls impaled on posts facing the river. The gruesome relics were tastefully decorated by a ruffle of palm leaves rolled into scrolls at the end, which maintained a shivering movement in the breeze. The skulls were provided with very long noses, more like long beaks, and the eye sockets were filled with clay and eyes made from small red seeds. They were painted with raddle and were indeed grinning caricatures of death.

The raised road of sticks follows parallel to the entire length of the long house and on its other side are arranged numerous irregular groups of houses. These are the abodes of the women. As we passed by, a few coyly left the small porticoed verandah in front to peer through cracks and crevices. The wives of all the male members of a family dwell in the one house and family life as we understand it does not exist.

The houses are rarely more than thirty or forty feet long and from the small door a narrow hallway leads the length to an exit at the opposite end. On either side small cubicles are arranged. The fires burn smokily, choking the acrid atmosphere.

The women were busy kneading sago, mixing it with mashed bananas and rolling the mixture into sausages with outer coverings of leaf. These they laid on the embers and baked. The staple diet smelt much

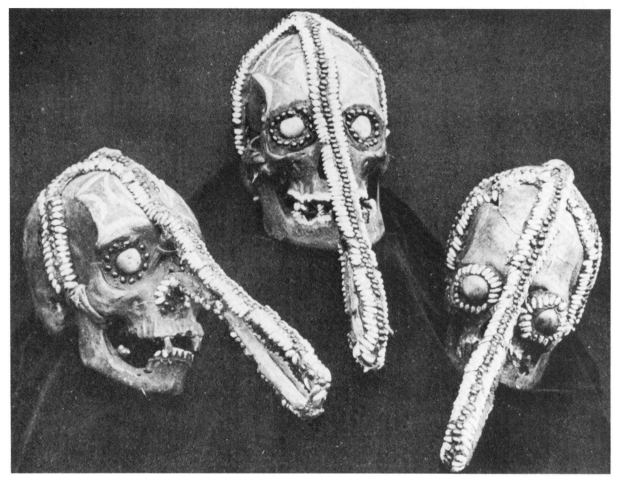

Three ornamented and preserved skulls in Papua

like burnt glue. On the walls hung fish traps and nets, while from the roof pended inverted cornucopia-like receptacles woven from fibre, for holding and parcelling up of sago. The women are brought like merchandise and become slaves to the indolent males. When the food was cooked they carried it to the long house where the hungry lords awaited.

Our next stopping place was Dopima, a village conspicuous because of the missionaries Chalmers and Tomkins, who while endeavouring to proselytize the people, were killed and eaten. We did not go ashore.

The following day we came suddenly upon a long house facing a fine beach of hard dark sand. The inmates were all idling, excepting a few old men making arrowheads, the points being shaped and barbed by the use of a mollusc shell. There was a particularly fine skull shrine near the entrance and I tried every possible ruse to secure it precisely as it stood. The son of the owner arrived and I displayed the purchase price before him – one axe, 100 sticks of tobacco, twenty pounds of rice, five ramis, five strings of beads, five white cowrie shells, five bidi-bidi (head of cone shells), one large knife, two large armshells. The son informed me that if he disposed of these things the sorcerers would kill him by puripuri! I placed a large and tempting bundle of armshells with the rest of my offerings. This was too much for the young fellow, who, without hesitation, acquiesced.

We continued towards Urama. It was a deep relief when the water widened into a broad expanse and the Urama villages came into view on a salient point. As usual the rattling out of the anchor was the signal for a flotilla of canoes to put off from shore. They seemed to dart from nowhere and yet come from everywhere; from the mangroves that overhung the waters from unseen creeks, down slimy mudbanks, tobogganing they poled ahead over the slime.

The impression conveyed was that the people were walking on water. As the canoes came closer they resolved themselves into hollowed out grooves, ten feet long and wide enough for a single figure to stand in. The hull was half round, devoid of outrigger, keel or stabilizing device of any kind except a rower who stood upright and propelled the extraordinary craft with long sweeps of a broad paddle. So deftly are the canoes handled they seem to become part of the paddler himself, the balance being maintained instinctively much as a bird on the wing. The environment of these people is water and ooze, and as their only means of moving about is by canoe, canoeing is as natural a process as walking.

A large canoe paddled by a crew of ten came out. In it were two elderly men plainly decorated but of a dignified presence that at once evinced authority. The village Chiefs were making their official call. Gormier was the War Chief and Coir the Village Chief who attended to village welfare and social affairs. I invited the dignitaries aboard and gave them presents of axes, tobacco and armshells which at once put us on good terms. We received a return invitation to visit the village, which we did without delay.

Soon we were on the threshold of the village, which owing to the falling tide was surrounded by mudflats several hundred yards wide. The crew put down their paddles, jumped overboard knee deep into the ooze and sledged the canoe along a mud groove up to the village. As we glided over the mud we scared myriads of tiny hopping fishes. Coir loudly announced our arrival in the village, a ceremony which proved an order for the women and children to flee to their homes and for the men to welcome us at the waterfront. They were a wild looking motley, famed on account of their warlike and independent nature and the failure of the authorities to subdue them. Even now the villages will have naught to do with missionaries, traders or labour recruiters. Certain of the missionaries influence the natives to abandon dances and customs allegedly evil. They are only evil by comparison, and what is given in return for the banishment of age-old customs is a spiritual teaching that has little compensation and lesser consolation for the natives.

Coir led the way through the village, which seemed deserted; but I heard feminine whisperings and titterings as we passed close to the huts, which convinced me that civilisation had not changed this trait of feminine nature. Coir stopped before a house, which had a large tassel of teased fibre dangling from the apex of its porch-like entrance. Then raising his voice he called 'Yarib! Yarib!' Immediately a not uncomely woman coyly appeared at the entrance, with two big brown-eyed infants. She wore the conventional pearl shell crescent; and a few strands of grass. Her hands were scored with hard labours and her feet were characteristically large, a natural evolution inherited from generations of mudwalkers.

Mrs Yarib Coir cast a not unkindly eye on the rows of beads around my neck and McCulloch's immaculate white legs. Accordingly I handed my interpreter

Coir, the Lord Mayor of Urama. Although he appears fierce and warlike in this picture, he was a mild, good-humoured fellow and unlike his dignified colleague Gormier, was vain and given to boastful chatter. In more civilized parts Coir would undoubtedly be designated a bore

several of the necklaces and asked him to present them to Mrs Yarib Coir from 'Woman belong me'. The brown lady became appreciably coquettish and disappeared into her house. Soon she returned with a tuft of at least a score of long grass strands. The raiment was presented to me with the translation, 'Woman belong Coir – make present Woman belong you'.

We trudged to the far end of the village which was bounded by a very oozy creek. On the far side rose several colossal temples – the Dubu Daimas or club houses of the men, which could only be reached by a frail bridge of doubtful construction. Coir's authority terminated by this moat. Beyond the bridge lay Gormier's province.

McCulloch and I carefully picked our way over the rotten slippery sticks and climbing up a crude ladderway stood on the threshold of a great arched porch that rose fifty feet above us. From the apex dangled a weird collection of amulets carved from wood. Human effigies, small crocodiles, lizards and other symbolic objects, which were to protect the house against the evil spirits of which they live in eternal dread. Bending low we passed through a ridiculously small doorway into the eerie gloom of an immense hall – a veritable palace of death. We stood in a large vestibule from which a wide hall extended the length of the temple to a door at the far end.

This vestibule was evidently the general assembly chamber. On either side of the hall entrance were two large racks filled with human skulls; beneath these racks pended 'Gope' plaques with wondrously carved faces no two of which were alike. These represented the ancestral spirits of the tribe; below these again and resting on the floor were rows of boar and crocodile skulls, probably trophies offered to the ancestral spirits. As we passed down the gloomy hall I noticed on either side small cubicles, each with its own skull shrine and ancestral spirit plaques, dark dens over which the very shadow of death seemed to brood.

At the far end the passage opened into another vestibule, on the opposite walls of which were skull racks and enormous Kaiva-Ku-Ku masks. Gormier indicated that this was his lavara or cubicle. The religion of the tribes is a combination of Manes or Ancestor worship and skull cult. So long as the ancestral plaques were attached to the enemies' skulls the latters' spirits were enslaved to the ancestral spirits in the next life, and the more enemies they killed in this life the more slaves they would have in the next.

A chief's skull-rack, with the heads of his enemies and their shields

A short distance from the warriors' Dubu were three smaller dubus, which were the compounds of the unmarried novitiates. On reaching pubic age they are transferred to isolation and spend their adolescence acquiring the tribal tenets and proving their manhood by ordeal. If a man is physically unable to endure the training he is ineligible for marriage.

I had a conference with Coir and Gormier as to the possibility of arranging a dance for the cinema on the morrow, and late in the night a canoe came out to our lugger and informed us that the dance had been arranged. Coir's voice could be heard haranguing the village and ordering all the women and children to clear out at daybreak. This was to be an esoteric

Frank Hurley surrounded by the trophies given to him to place in the white men's club house

performance which only the initiated might behold! Before break of day, the obedient spouses left the village and a long trail of canoes, laden with women, children and dogs filed out into the river into a bush waterway.

Everyone was putting on feathers, shell ornaments and decorating with raddle. At the landing a wonderfully decorated crowd formed a guard of honour, and Coir conducted us through lines of warriors to the Dubu Daima. A great commotion of dancers and chanting was going on inside. The chant was led by Gormier, who piped in a highly pitched falsetto, and presently the whole assembly of dancers took up the theme in chorus.

A couple of hundred dancers arranged in long lines down the length of the hallway, the light from the doorway glinting on decorations and glistening eyes, diffused half light faintly throwing into relief the setting of great Kaiva-Ku-Ku masks, grotesquely carved Gope, and the eyeless sockets of the skulls. The drums tommed, the massed voices chorused and each figure moved in the rhythm with the whole. The white feathers swayed with each movement of the head; the head-dresses of Cassowary danced, the elbow plumes danced – even the house jigged.

The dance appeared to proceed in short sets – each differing from the other only in slight alteration of chant. The village chief, Coir, and his understudy performed the very wicked and realistic dance of the witch doctors. As the men had the village entirely to themselves I inquired whether the Kaiva-Ku-Ku masks might not promenade for our benefit. After much deliberation they assented.

The warriors arranged themselves in a circle and squatted down chanting and drumming. The Kaiva-Ku-Ku came from out of the Dubu, and danced in short jumpy steps into the centre of the ring of swaying bodies and heads. Then began a series of shuffling caperings, the masked dancers, facing one another, drawing apart, intertwining and ringing with an intricate complexity. The ceremony is a celebration of the initiation of new members into the brotherhood of the tribe: but we could ascertain nothing definite from Gormier who was in honour bound not to divulge the inner secrets of the Dubu.

I made council in the Dubu, and started preliminary negotiations for the purchase of a complete skull rack of twenty-four skulls, the Gope shields pending beneath it and the pig skulls, which were arranged in a long row at the bottom. I said that we white men were travelling over the length and breadth of New Guinea, learning the customs and ways of its people and collecting their arts and crafts. Beyond New Guinea was a great world where the white people came from with enormous Dubus made of stone wherein all things belonging to the native people all over the world are kept for all time. When Gormier and his people were dead the trophies we would collect would live on, and memories of them would never be forgotten.

I said I should like to take the whole partition from the Dubu, skull rack and all, and would erect it exactly as it stood in the Great Dubu of the Whitemen. He could not give me his rack of skulls – they were the inheritance of his children and must be passed on: but he would help me. He took from the rack one of his best skulls. He untied one of the Gope from its setting and selected one of the largest pig skulls and placed them beside me. Gormier then called the names of the warriors individually. They entered their small cubicles and did as he did.

The little bundles were all brought and laid down on the floor of Gormier's cubicle. On each I placed a knife, twenty-two sticks of tobacco, six bidi-bidi and one armshell. They tore fibre from the Dubu decorations and helped to pack the skulls and tie up the Gope. I expressed a wish to have a rack made exactly similar to Gormier's. The old men went away and late in the evening the rack was brought out complete in infinite detail, even to the crude little decorations of queer figures and totemic symbols. Daybreak and a full tide enabled us to pass over the shallow bank by the village and take a shorter route to the open sea. While it was still scarcely light our friends collected along the waterfront, and sent one of their canoes ahead to guide us through the intricate passage. As we turned into the daybreak stillness of a jungle waterway the last farewells died from my ears, 'Ba-ma-huta! Ba-ma-huta!'

THE LATEST MONSTER VISITS HANAUABADE

Port Moresby is the gateway to Papua and the head-quarters of the Administration. It differs little from other townships of far North Australia excepting in degree of ugliness and discomfort. The mosquitos are thoroughly healthy and one need not be excessively

The latest miracle of the wonder-working white man arrives in Elevala. For days following the arrival of the Seagull, *all work was suspended while the entire community gathered to discuss the 'canoe that flew like a bird'. Every native boy soon possessed a model of it made with astounding skill from light cottonwood*

scared of contracting malaria from their multifarious bites. The officials are as numerous and as healthy as the mosquitoes, and just as active.

It was from Port Moresby that we launched the expedition which ended at Lake Murray among the remote Sambio tribes who had never before seen a white man. Our sea-planes were the first machines ever seen in the Port and marked a third epoch in the history of the ancient Hanauabade village. Three times it had been startled from a primitive quiet by the wonders of the white men. . . . First the arrival of great ships propelled by gigantic sails as big as the sails of all the native canoes sewn together in one piece. Secondly, when a monstrous ship of iron entered the harbour, throwing from tall chimneys showers of smoke and sparks, and now a gigantic bird ushering in the era of aviation.

The planes arrived by steamer and were lowered from the deck into the water. As they slipped over the side, the natives gave throat to prolonged war whoops and smote the sides of their canoes with their paddles, producing a deep noted 'boom'. The testing of the engine, its deep throated roar, and propeller shimmering a transparent halo, sweeping the sea with its slip-stream in whirlwind sprays, scared them, but the natives were very sceptical about our capacity to make puripuri sufficiently powerful to raise the machine into the air.

The *Seagull* speeded in triumph, and cleaving aside the sea in frisky exultation, like a graceful bird that skips the crests before taking wing, rose into the air. Not a word fell from the onlookers. They seemed as if hypnotised by the preternatural, until, like a whirlwind blast that wrecks all within its path, the machine headed directly towards them. Yells of terror, and the song of the *Seagull* sounded over the town. The native servants fled from the houses, the court was forcefully adjourned, as prisoners, plaintiffs and police rushed for the open. The prisoners bolted from the gaol, the frothing tankard was forgotten.

Lang circled the town, and then glided to the sea with the elegant grace of a seagull. He was regarded as either a god or a devil, and the sea-plane became an object of awe and reverence. All work in the community had to be abandoned for days, because the natives would not return, but insisted upon spending their time discussing the extraordinary machine and the success of the undertaking. But not one evinced any desire to make a flight. 'Canoe stop-along water, more safe,' they said, grinning from ear to ear. 'He very slow, but we get there by-and-by all the same.'

KAIMARI, A VILLAGE OUT OF THE PREHISTORIC WORLD
STRANGE RITES AND STRANGER IMAGES

Kaimari is one of the largest of the Purari Delta villages. Looking down one thousand feet from the sea-plane the village appears more like a floating collection of thatched houseboats when the tide is high. At low water, or rather high mud, Kaimari is a place of oozy desolation. Kaimari is midway between Port Moresby and the Fly River Delta from where we planned our entrance into the swampy and unexplored interior. Lang and I came by sea-plane from the Port along the coast.

The climate is that of a prehistoric world in which the land appears to be still in the process of emerging from a vast ocean. It rains constantly and in the rare moments when it is not raining the air is filled with a thick mist. The river itself seems one of liquid mud. The entire delta is a vast swamp. Portions of it appear only when the receding tide reveals mud flats on which the natives perch precarious dwellings. The vegetation is thick and heavy, and the tangle of mangroves eternally drips moisture.

The *Eureka* had arrived a few hours previously and as we slowly taxied up to the vessel, forty large canoes, filled with warriors, put off from the shore

The Eureka, *in which Frank Hurley made his voyage*

and began excitedly circling the *Seagull*, beating the canoe sides with their paddles until the noise sounded like the rumbling of thunder. The warriors were completely fearless and it was with great difficulty that we kept them from ramming the seaplane and being cut to pieces by the propeller.

Shortly after our arrival, the chiefs made their official call. The old gents were heavily encumbered about their necks with dogs' teeth and shells, their sole garments. In their wake followed a fleet of canoes laden to the gunwales with enthusiastic and strong-smelling warriors. They came on behalf of the village people to make a peace offering of a pig to the 'Canoe belonga two fella God'. Amid great ceremony, the sacrifice was brought out toward sunset and placed reverently on the altar-like bow of the seaplane.

The main thoroughfare of Kaimari is a raised roadway of mangrove sticks that runs the length of the village and spans creeks and slime in rickety rottenness. From it, pathways ramify to the domiciles, and so the inhabitants are able to move about without sinking thigh-deep in filth. A low fence extends around the waterfront which keeps the crocodiles without and the pigs within – sometimes.

On the mud flat before the fence lie stranded large numbers of the characteristic Purari canoes – excavated logs varying in length up to forty-five feet. The bow is cut so low that when heavily laden a small boy squats there, and is caulked in with mud. Little 'stick-in-the-mud' keeps out the bow wave, whilst a narrow barrier of mud seals off the wake astern.

Kaimari mud has a thousand uses. It is the playground where the pigs and children revel and wallow. It is the field where the staple foods, crabs and sago, thrive. In fact the whole place is an odoriferous quagmire, from which the populace seem moulded. A canoe may be navigated either by one old woman, who sits in the stern and with a large flat paddle directs the barque as it drifts with the current, or by a dozen stalwart young warriors with swelling muscles

and rhythmic swing that stem their craft defiantly against the press of tide or stream. As the only means of moving from place to place is by canoe, the youngest children are as adroit afloat as they are nimble in balancing and hopping about the treacherous saplings of the Promenade.

The Kaimari ladies are the most unbeautiful creatures I have seen. Their dress, microscopically speaking, is customary rather than effective. The hair is shorn close, leaving a narrow ridge down the centre, and two rings above the ears resemble tufts of

Portrait of a native wearing full dress: the bone nose ornament is worn only on occasions of great importance

astrakan. Fashions in coiffure are variable, and the design might riot to a knob fore and aft, or a ridge athwart the cranium. In others the hair covers the scalp in small sprouts as if sown. Eyes are unusually goo-goo (probably on account of the eyebrows having been plucked out), and as scandalous as the broad nose with its pierced septum and six-inch nasal decoration. Lips thick and framing a mighty red orifice displaying two rows of black teeth – discoloured by the habitual chewing of betel nut and lime.

A few straggling coconuts struggle for existence in the less submerged mud areas, but nothing else does well about the village but mangroves, death and decay. Hunched up by her doorway sits an old woman plastered in mud from head to toe. Her shrivelled body is encumbered with skeins and cables of native cords. Her limbs are bound with ligatures until the flesh stands out. She mourns her husband and does penance for his death. On another verandah squats a group of garrulous freaks – females that resemble moving mud casts. They are all in mourning. Perhaps a distant relative or a dog. These people appear to have absorbed the inexpressible gloom that permeates even the weeping skies; and each evening as darkness falls the thunder growls about these hapless people of gloom and storm.

We advance to a colossal building whither the path leads and ends. Across the imposing entrance stretches a barrier of woven palm leaf, with a flap obscuring the door. The great arch culminates seventy feet above us. We stood on the threshold of a great hall that extended like a vast cavern to a remote gloom. On the floor some forty or fifty sleeping forms snored their afternoon siesta. From roof and walls pended an amazing collection of fantastic masks in various stages of construction. A particularly repulsive old gentleman, much decorated with dog's teeth and evidently the chief, assigned himself to showing us around, which he did with great ostentation and jabber. A crowd of men followed us through the Ravi, the name of these great Purari club-houses.

For three hundred feet we walked along an aisle, with the heavy constructional poles on either side. These poles, as well as supporting the roof, marked the limits of lavara or cubicles which contained numbers of remarkably carved plaques, probably representing ancestral spirits. Beneath these 'Kwoi' plaques were heaps of crocodile, pig and occasional human skulls, doubtless heirlooms and trophies. We then came to a partition that barred further progress. Only the chief and we two white men proceeded.

Squeezing through a narrow opening we were in an apartment some fifty feet in length by fifteen in width: the roof had tapered from the entrance, and was now only ten feet high. Grouped closely together were seventeen wild and eerie effigies, the sacred and dread Kopiravi. These grotesque objects were reminiscent caricatures of crocodiles yawning heartily. They stood on four legs of cassowary design and had an opening in the belly so that a man might stand erect therein and carry them about. Until recently the mangled bodies of victims were thrust into the gaping jaws of these implacable gods as offerings; in the morning the bodies were removed and cut up for the ghoulish feast. On emerging from the chamber of horrors, the old chief truculently demanded Ku-Ku (tobacco) and intimated that unless we gave and appeased the wrath of the Kopiravi a serious calamity or sickness would befall us; so we gave.

The old men are an astute lot of impostors and hypocrites, and I suspected that the motive of the Kopiravi is to terrorize the young men, women and children. The prestige of these old men is an interesting manifestation of the reverence for priests and the priest-cult which exists in some degree or other throughout the world, and is invariably strong among primitive peoples who have a reverence for magic, medicine men, and puripuri, as the Papuans designate the supernatural. By the use of the mystic Kopiravi masks and by quantities of similar paraphernalia, the elders succeed in keeping the women, young men and children under complete control. If

The sacred masks used by the older men of the tribe to exert influence over the villagers and inspire great terror

there occurs a shortage in the crop of coconuts, a tabu is placed upon the fruit. Word is given out by the dotards that to eat the coconut during a designated period will produce terrible illness and death. The result is that nothing could induce a woman, child or a young man even to touch a coconut during this period; but the fruit disappears all the same. Someone eats it. The old men put the blame upon the spirits.

Likewise, a young hunter, having shot a pig, is required to bring it as an offering to the spirits who inhabit the awful cell at the far end of the Ravi. Like the coconuts, the pig disappears. The spirits, it seems, have only a taste for those things which are considered delicacies by the inhabitants of these delta villages.

A FLIGHT THROUGH A WORLD OF MUD, CLOUD AND RAIN FROM KAIMARI TO DARU IN A TROPIC STORM

The next stage was the most hazardous of the expedition, the passage by air and water to Daru.

Our farewell to Kaimari was exceptionally dramatic. The whole population assembled by the waterfront to see us off, and as the *Seagull* taxied from her moorings, wild cries of, 'Keyamo! Keyamo!' (goodbye) sounded above the roar of the engine.

All went well until we reached a point off the southern extremity of Kiwai, an attenuated ribbon of silt called an island, which lies midway across the Fly estuary and splits the furious tides. An ominous bank of towering cumuli was drifting in rapidly from the east with a deluge streaming from its under surface. Heavy rain and scud clouds obscured Kiwai, save the extreme southern point. We just cleared the passage between the storms, fully expecting the way to be barred by lightning which was flickering among the clouds in the vicinity. All we experienced was a violent tossing from the breath of the storm that puffed at us as we escaped from its clutches.

Still the reaper chased behind through blinding rain and mist, and almost clutched our tail as we fled through the narrow Parama passage between Brampton Island and the mainland. In half a minute we fell from 1,500 feet to 300 feet, and still were falling rapidly. Then an upcurrent heaved us up three hundred feet, and the machine was almost overturned and began to slip sideways; when it seemed that we must inevitably kill many crabs on the mudbanks, we righted and were through Hell's gates. We made a broad sweep over Daru, and then descended bumpily on to the crest of the rollers, for a big sea was driving in. The *Seagull* was anchored on a mudflat in the lee of the pier on which the entire white population, numbering fully seven, gathered to welcome us.

Daru is one of the most outcast and isolated spots in the world – an insignificant silt inlet set in a tawny sea which nature has compassionately hidden by dense mangrove jungles and a species of eucalyptus. The white population comprises four officials, one missionary and two residents. A bygone magistrate did much to improve the place by planting magnificent hedges of gay foliaged crotons and these alone make the place tenable. Mosquitoes are an irksome irritation but it is doubtful which harasses the white intruder the most – the mosquitoes, the officials or the missionary – or which irritates the community itself most.

Lang, Hill and Williams remained at Daru, to overhaul the *Seagull* before making a further flight into the interior. The rest of the party sailed across the Torres Straits to Thursday Island to overhaul our wireless apparatus.

UP A TROPIC RIVER INTO THE UNKNOWN ADURU AND THE UNTAMED, LONELY PARADISE BEYOND

3 January. We left Daru at 10.45 a.m. just as the tide was beginning to run out, and headed across the

shallows for Tauru Passage. Once through we turned north and entered the muddy waters of the Fly Estuary, which at the mouth is about forty miles wide. Entering is like sailing on an inland sea. This mighty stream, though but 500 to 600 miles in length, is said to pour into the sea as much water as the Amazon. At evening we dropped anchor off the little village of Daware. It appears to be the only half acre of dry land hereabouts; the rest is mangrove and eternal swamp.

4 January. Islands are frequently being washed away, others made, while the river continually alters its channel. Shoals come into being, and in the next flood the entire topography might be altered again. The river banks are still covered by jungles of mangroves with an occasional small village on the infrequent high bank.

At 1.00 p.m. we dropped anchor at a plantation known as Mediri, the only plantation for over 200 miles around. The single figure of a white man looks inexpressibly lonely and outcast in this dreary place. We carried a small mail and half side of bacon for Mr Beach, who greeted us warmly; we were the first white men he had seen for months. He is married and has one daughter, Frances, ten years of age.

The plantation impressed me as a failure. The soil is much too clayey and heavy to produce coconuts and the rain is excessive. The rubber trees were lean and sapling-like, though they have been planted for seven years. The area of the plantation is 400 acres, and it is a mystery how it produces sufficient revenue to warrant keeping it going. Fortunately the venture is a missionary industrial one, and dividends are not such an important matter as if the plantation was worked on private capital.

Beach has been at many things in his time – a recruiter, bird collector, prospector and other vocations which a ne'er-do-well might take up in these parts. He is, however, a strong and kindly character. We dined at his bungalow, a fine large house made of native materials.

Five o'clock in the afternoon is always an event at Mediri – Mrs Beach feeds the fowls and animals. The food is principally shredded coconut, and the cats and dogs and feathery flocks all in one wild scramble mingle together in the evening repast. Then there are duels between cats and hens – and cockfights and much noise of cackling, meowing and barking; but beyond this the ceaseless routine of the plantation, the interminable rain, mud and isolation. Yet Beach is resigned to it; he has accepted the wild for his home and mate and is wedded to it.

8 November. At daylight we were under way to Kaled Island. Two canoes came out from the shore and we entered into friendly relations with the natives who indicated that their village, Aduru, lay on the far bank.

Their canoes are unexcelled throughout the Territory for the excellence of their workmanship, being up to fifty feet long and beautifully excavated. The outrigger is secured to the dugout by two slender distance pieces, or poles, which are fastened to the outrigger by a number of slender struts. These latter are so arranged as to prevent movement laterally or longitudinally. The whole arrangement is light and possessed of great strength. The vessel might be considered graceful and elegant. The paddlers sit on small cane crosspieces which are bound onto the top sides of the canoe. The vessel is kept in motion by short rapid strokes, and can maintain readily the speed of our vessel against the current and in spurts readily pass us. We are capable of making a speed of six knots. We went ashore, with cameras, benzine tins, beads, tobacco and expectations.

We made our way along the narrow path by the creek and up the stairs railed by bannisters. We went in through a small opening and found ourselves in an acrid gloom through which phantom figures moved hither and thither. The forms resolve themselves into hideous furies, moving about among great heaps of bananas, and feast stuffs. These fearful crones are the women of the village, unbeautiful beyond belief.

Some time ago, a notable man in the village died, and since then the people have covered themselves with sackcloth and ashes; but the ashes in this case happened to be the ooze of the Fly and the sackcloth garments of teased out grasses which wreathed the unfortunate females in hideous shrouds. This strange mourning garb is girdled about the body, completely covering the breasts like a corselet. It clasps the waist and then falls down in long tresses behind. The horrible aspect is increased by caps which fit the head closely and flow away in a profusion of combed out fibre which falls behind to mingle with the grass train of the mourning garment. As if these encumbrances were not sufficient, their bodies were heavily bedaubed with the mud of the Fly. I pitied these wretched moving bundles of grass and mud, for the heat was well nigh unbearable and I learned that they had been wearing this shroud of penance for a whole season!

The crafts of the natives show them to have attained to a fair stage of development. Their basketwork is unexcelled throughout the Territory and shows conspicuous originality in ornament and design. The fishing nets and hoop nets are admirable.

The chief game of the small boys seems to be the fun of splashing each other with mud, for each morning they collect on the flat in front of the village and engage in the strange pastime.

Another item of interest was the smoking. Firstly the tobacco is shredded and dried by holding an ember close above it; the cigarette is then rolled, a leaf being used in lieu of paper, which is then inserted in a long bamboo holder and the lighted end is placed in the mouth. The vigorous exhaling of the breath blows the smoke out of the open end of the holder which is at once inserted in the hole of the smoke reservoir made from a section of bamboo. This exhaling is continued until the smoke issues freely from a second hole in the reservoir. This latter is then passed around and the inhaling is done by merely drawing the smoke from either of the reservoir holes. Two or three deep inhalations appear ample to produce a sense of dopiness and to the uninitiated, suffocation.

10 January. It is 150 miles to Lake Murray with a strong current against us all the way. The river banks are like wondrous stage settings. . . . Mammoth trees overwhelmed by vines carrying great burdens of orchids and countless epiphyte growths. . . . Each plant, tree and vine strives for a chance to live and bring forth its seed. Great trees formed the hosts for countless parasitic growths which flourished so profusely as to completely hide the form of the parent tree. . . . Over the calm waters, lit by the blaze of an equatorial sun, myriads of horseflies and butterflies danced. Birds of Paradise, hornbills, Goura pigeons and other dazzling flocks of gorgeous plumage flew overhead or sang amid the vines. . . .

12 January. Cassowary Island. . . . The river banks reminiscent of old castles and ruins covered with vines. The entire trees overwhelmed by cascades and festoons of marvellous creepers making many fanciful forms . . . a region of fairy castles, where beauty slept everywhere and only the droning purr of our exhaust broke the enchantment.

The Paradise bird – they glint and flash out into the sunshine, then careen back to the gloom of the jungle, which thrills with their characteristic notes. Cassowary Island is an immense camp of flying foxes. They perch like birds, then as the wings are closed, gravitation comes into action and over they go, pending from the branches head down. . . .

14 January. Entered the Strickland at 10.45 a.m., at what is known as Everill Junction.

15 January. All day forcing the passage of the Strickland, navigating as far as possible in the lee side of points and bends and thus avoiding a great percentage of the current. At 3.00 p.m. entered the Herbert River, quite an unobtrusive stream which is the outlet of Lake Murray. It is still another one hundred miles before the mountains are reached.

16 January. Continued passing up the course of the Herbert. The keenest expectation on board as to the

nature of the Lake and its strange mysteries. . . . Then the trees along the banks dwindled away to reeds and over the top of the swamps the distant ramifying waters of this extraordinary inland sea. One canoe in the remote distance, the first human life seen since leaving Aduru on the Fly estuary, 200 miles away!

MEN OUT OF THE STONE AGE
'THE LOST TRIBES' AND THE EMPTY WORLD
OF LAKE MURRAY

I decided not to enter the lake by night, knowing nought of its uncharted waters, and having been previously informed as to the treachery of the natives. Across the waters came the tom-tom of drums; the frogs chorused an anthem from the swamps, and the eerie cry of night-birds made the air pregnant with mystery and enchantment.

As the curtain of dawn was raised our boys were entering the portals of the lake, and the fantastic outlines of a great house came into view – the citadel of the head-hunters. The anchor chain rattled out and we came to rest, crying, 'Sambio! Sambio! Sambio!' the sole word which we knew of the lake-dwellers' language. But the only answer was the echo that travelled through the deserted house. As nothing appeared to be stirring, the *Eureka* was nosed inshore, and accompanied by McCulloch and four of the most trusty of my native crew, I went ashore in the dinghy to make our official call.

We pushed up the narrow track that led between the tall reeds, until further progress was barred by arrows thrust in the ground and a skull impaled on a pole. This we could scarcely interpret as a hospitable welcome. I substituted a green bough, red calico and presents, emblematic of peace.

The village comprised a single immense house, 350 feet long, fifty feet wide and thirty-five feet high to the apex of the arched entrance with the roof projecting in a tapering snout, symbolizing a crocodile *couchant*

with jaws a-yawn. The ridge-pole projected an additional twelve feet and was split at the end, beak-like, and a human thigh-bone thrust in transversely suggesting the armorial bearings of the tribe. There were eleven small openings on either side, which led to small cubicles. The main porch was apparently reserved exclusively for the fighting men, whilst the women and children occupied the smaller cubicles.

A warning skull greets the intruders

The floor of the main portico was divided into rectangles by laying down and lashing transversely heavy saplings. Each space was allotted to the fighting males of a family, who slept on the bare ground, coiled close to the smouldering embers to avoid mosquitoes, or squatted on the saplings during the day, grinding their stone axes, fashioning arrowheads from bones with flint gouges, and chewing betel nut. At convenient points hooked uprights were placed where the bows, arrows, and stone clubs were hung in constant readiness. From the rafters pended gruesome war trophies of human skulls and souvenirs of the chase. Truly it was a model dwelling out of the Stone Age.

The family section was partitioned off from the warriors' den by sago frond stems lashed together, and consisted of two rows of dismal pens fenced off by low barriers. Each was provided with a raised platform for sleeping and a small doorway into the open. We had entered the Stygian home of prehistoric swamp-dwellers living by the shores of a primeval sea. In the pens warm embers still remained; the belongings hung from the rafters in countless bags. One grass bag contains a full dress – the height of prehistoric fashion – a chic grass mode that begins at the waist and ends at the knees. This one is a baby's cradle. Mother just places him within the knitted bag, and suspends him to rock from the nearest pole. This large one – it swarms with earwigs, scorpions, cockroaches, and spiders – contains lots of small grass-plaited pouches.

In a dim alcove treasures beyond: bonanza! Human heads! Stuffed heads! The heads had been severed from the victims, preserving the neck as long as possible; the skin had been split up the back of the neck to the cranium, and the brain and all fleshy parts extracted by mascerating in water and scraping with a bamboo knife. The skin had been replaced on the skull and stuffed with coconut fibre. The native taxidermist then sewed it up at the back. The stuffing process distorted the face longitudinally, whilst the mouth which was forced open excessively was stopped with a ball of clay. The eyes were likewise treated and decorated with red seeds. The whole gruesome object had evidently been subjected to a lengthy smoke-curing process which mummified it and stopped decay. Finally the trophy was decorated with Iconic designs executed in red and yellow ochre and a large seed was found in the brain cavity – which evidently caused much grim amusement when shaken as a rattle during their death dances. What sort of people could these be that so callously made toys of their victims?

Our friendly efforts to draw the natives from the jungle met with no success. The only signs of human life on the entire lake were great fires kindled at several remote points. We turned our energies to exploring the lake in search of other villages hoping that the invisible savages would at last meet our friendly overtures and come into the open.

Two days later we found ourselves anchored close to a village. In the dusk of the evening before, it had been so well camouflaged as to deceive even the powerful binoculars. For the sake of security and a means of escape, if necessary, we sailed close to the shore and there launched the dinghy.

SAMBIO!! SAMBIO!!

We discovered many fresh tracks. The inhabitants had left in a great hurry – perhaps when the rising dawn revealed our ship close at hand on the lake. The embers were still warm and the pigs were still in the pen. We left behind a few yards of gaudy coloured fabric and a couple of axes, heaved anchor and turned our course back into the lake. Scarcely had we progressed two miles when I noticed through the glasses a pair of canoes, one being paddled by eight men. The other seemed to be towed. The *Eureka* began rapidly to gain and the two canoes begin to draw apart. One appeared to be abandoned while the other rowed frantically for the bank. As we drew close to the abandoned canoe, I observed it to be filled with stuffed heads, stone axes, bows, arrows, and all the sundries appertaining to the Lake Murray village.

I remained on the platform waving frantically a piece of yellow fabric and calling out, 'Sambio!! Sambio!!' After much deliberation the canoe began to row slowly toward us, while both the paddlers and myself continued to shout, 'Sambio! Sambio!' These men put down their bows and arrows and approached us, knowing neither their fate nor our intentions, but relying solely upon the honour of that magic word, 'Sambio!'

When they came alongside they fulfilled all the grotesque and fanciful ideas we had formed of them. Truly they were prehistoric creatures – practically nude, covered by the hideous sipuma skin, and having the most amazing features. Their voices, strange to say, were pleasantly euphonious. The cast of feature is amazingly Hebraic. Indeed, were it not for the deep bronze of their skins, they might have passed for one of the Lost Tribes of Israel bronzed Babylonian Jews. The hair is shorn off close in the front; but the back extends in a long cluster of luxuriant pigtails which are increased in length by plaiting them with fibre.

We made friends and began active trading. I demonstrated the power of the rifle and its accuracy. At the report most of them jumped overboard in terror. What astonished them more than the actual report or the carrying distance of the bullet was the echo. It reverberated for fully thirty seconds and it was clear that they thought it was the shot still travelling. Matches, the taste of salt and of sugar, alike astonished and pleased them; but what they clamoured for were the empty tins which we had saved for the purpose – empty oil and benzine tins. These primitive folk are entirely destitute of utensils of any description beyond bamboo and a few water baskets made by folding the sheath of the Goru palm.

Papuan chieftain

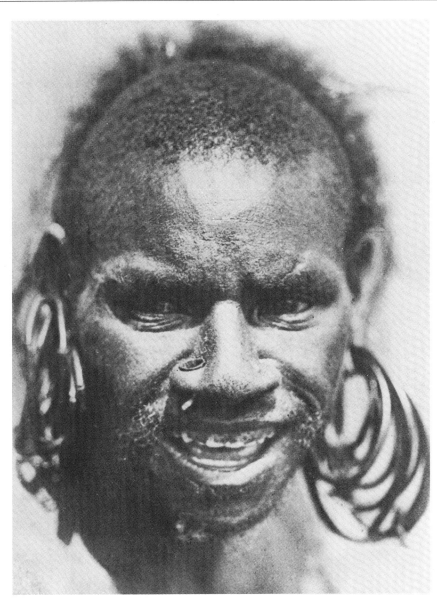

A Papuan man catches sight of himself reflected
in the lens of the camera

For a few tins we purchased a bundle of arrows, paddles, stone clubs and other implements. They were also eager to secure axes and knives. After trading to our advantage and their satisfaction, they directed us with great zeal to their village. We took the canoe in tow, an event which caused among the paddlers the greatest hilarity and delight. We landed to a wild song and dance to which the warriors beat time on drums and benzine tins, while others shook violently stuffed human heads which emitted a not unpleasant rattling.

There were some fifty warriors but to my consternation neither women nor children. This is ever an ominous sign and presages trouble. As we loitered on the foreshore the chief seemed to sense the reason for my hesitancy and motioned the warriors away. As they departed into the jungle immediately behind the village, I noticed them snatch up bows and arrows from the concealment of the grass. With rifles at the ready we followed the chief in single file along a narrow track towards the house.

The chief motioned us to enter but my native bodyguard warned me against this ruse. Once inside the darkness of the Dubu, a signal would have brought the warriors from their concealment, we would have been surrounded and clubbed to death. Fifty bowmen were excitedly waiting the signal. We could hear their suppressed whispers coming from the jungle. It was some hundred paces back to the dinghy. The retreat would have to be made diplomatically.

I pointed to three fine specimens of stuffed human heads and in the language of signs, intimated that I wanted them and would pay six steel axes therefor. Six axes! Steel axes! I noticed the Hebraic shrewdness for a bargain sparkle in his eyes. I also intimated by signs that we would return after the axes were brought from the vessel. So he was going to get six axes in addition to six heads! The shrewd old man called something back to his followers and carried the heads back along the track to the dinghy. He would wait on the foreshore for our return.

From then on we decided not to land but to do our work from the vessel. The only means of landing involved some way of terrifying the people and this I had no desire to do. As if nothing had happened, the canoes put off from the shore the next morning and paid us a visit. I paid over the axes and this served to inspire confidence and to renew the friendship. Other canoes remained inshore at some distance, probably as reinforcements and to see what happened to their emissaries. We treated them in a friendly fashion and soon the balance of the fleet joined their braver fellows. I noticed that these people were practically without weapons of defence, having left them ashore. I lost no time in getting busy with my camera and after great coaxing and persuasion, induced one of the party to come aboard and 'pose'.

He was unusually fidgety and not at all an easy subject. Presently the sitter noticed his reflection in the lens, and became alarmed. It required many 'sambios' to reassure him. I also allowed him to view his fellows through the reflex camera. This seemed to kindle an unimaginative intelligence, and I was able to secure an exposure. As there were many diverse types I kept our decoy on board to reassure the others, but they were all very nervous and I was forced to make quick exposures. Most of them were of a markedly Semitic type of countenance, while others resembled early Egyptians, an impression imparted doubtless by the strange manner of dressing the hair. The chief was decidedly an aristocratic type; with his crown of paradise plumes he might well have passed for a reincarnation of Solomon.

To observe their movements, I permitted the canoes a start and then heaved anchor and followed. They paddled in very close to the river bank and occasionally snatched bundles from the reeds. These I discovered were bundles of arrows which they had hidden, an act altogether excusable as a precaution of defence.

On the shore they began a fantastic song and dance to the accompaniment of a large drum and a half-

Under the Sea

John Williamson was born on the day his father was navigating his ship under double-reef topsails around Cape Horn – and his life was to be as exciting and as varied as his adventurous parent's. In fact, as Williamson later recalled, it was nearly three years before his father returned and 'cast his seafaring eye on the trim of my rigging'. But then it was little more than a glance, for his father carried with him his latest invention, 'It might have been a perpetual motion machine, but lo and behold, when he opened it up, it was a perfect folding baby carriage – a collapsible perambulator'. In this the infant Williamson was wheeled round the busy port of Liverpool.

The Williamson family had come from Scotland, and was soon on the move again – to America, where Williamson senior was building a hotel and a dam up in the mountains of Vermont. But before long they were drawn back to the sea and shipping at Norfolk, Virginia. Here the young Williamson dreamed of and very nearly did go to sea in a great white sailing ship. Instead, when he was sixteen he started a five-year marine draughtsman's apprenticeship, 'getting acquainted with every rivet and gadget from truck to keel'. Apprenticeship completed, he heard 'the lure of the West' and joined a touring minstrel show. In Denver he decided to become a newspaper cartoonist, and went to still-life classes.

However, he went back to the sea in Virginia, working on local papers as cartoonist, reporter, and photographer:

The routine was easy, but reaching the high point of perfection was not. The only remedy I knew was to put in heartless hours. Twenty hours a day was the usual thing, but it was just to my liking. . . . Often when through for the day I figured that the few hours for sleep might just as well be spent at the office, and would wake up with my feet under the drawing board. If trying hard would bring perfection, I was slowly, if not surely, on my way somewhere in that direction when my story opens.

Portrait of J. E. Williamson, inventor of the photo sphere and underwater photography

55

SUBMARINE ADVENTURES AND UNDERSEA FILM-MAKING, 1913, by John Williamson

THE FIRST PICTURES OUT OF THE DEPTHS

A newspaper man on the hunt for news might best describe my state of being as I stepped, one day, into a magic world that later became a reality. It happened in the old seaport of Norfolk, Virginia. I had strolled down a narrow street with the sea and ships at its end. Long, mysterious shadows filled the space between the ancient buildings looming ghostly and unreal against the glow of the setting sun. Silence reigned. The place seemed utterly deserted and forgotten. Above the crooked roofs and sagging chimneys was a fathomless green sky, and a strange sensation of standing on the bottom of the sea among the ruins of some sunken city came to me. I knew it was visionary, but I had always been fascinated by the legend of the lost Atlantis, and by the tales of known sunken cities of Yucatan and the submerged Port Royal in Jamaica. Standing there in the weird half-light of a dying day, I visualised these cities once peopled by humans and now the haunts of creatures of the sea. What wondrous stories they held. What astounding pictures they would present if photographed. Perhaps there would be wrecked ships, loaded treasure galleons, rotting in the silence of the once busy streets. I was seized with a sudden inspiration to make photographs of the world beneath the sea; that it had never been done made the idea more alluring.

Yet I might never have achieved my goal, or even thought of the idea, had it not been for an invention which my father, Captain Charles Williamson, after a lifetime of seafaring, had devised. He was just perfecting his marvellous deep-sea salvaging device, a flexible metal tube capable of reaching great depths. The tube made easy access to the sea floor, and thick green-glass ports allowed the occupant of the work chamber at the bottom a somewhat restricted view of undersea surroundings, enabling him to direct and operate giant grapples and arms when working on sunken wrecks. Herein lay the solution of my problem. I descended in the tube, and crouched in my photographic chamber, spent the afternoon 'at home' with the fishes thirty feet below the surface of the bay. Over and over again, I focused my camera and pressed the shutter, filled with tense excitement, nerves a-tingle. Would my experiment be a success? I watched the silver emulsion darkening under the action of the chemicals in the little red light of my dark room, and little by little, the outline of the fishes appeared. Finally, the whole scene stood out clearly in all its pristine beauty. Instantly I realised the tremendous importance of this achievement. If undersea photographs could be made at the speed I had used, then motion pictures could be made under similar conditions. 'Movies' meant magic even in 1913, when the industry was in its infancy and had not yet learned to talk.

The first account of my undersea photography published in the *Virginian Pilot* aroused unbounded interest throughout the world. Hundreds of letters and telegrams came in a flood as a result of that first account. Among them was a telegram inviting me to come to New York and exhibit my pictures at the First International Motion Picture Exposition, which was about to open at the Grand Central Palace. With my half-dozen four-by-five negatives, a few prints, and the papers with my plans in my pockets, I hurried to New York to accept the invitation. Among the enlargements I had made was one six feet wide, coloured with a sponge, which crowned the pictorial display that filled my booth at the opening of the Exposition. The picture of that patch of sea bottom with its fishes, just a few square yards of the vast ocean's floor, proved one of the greatest attractions of the show.

Money was all important. An expedition to the West Indies to invade Neptune's realm with a camera would be costly; and I realised that only in the crystal clear waters of the tropics would it be possible to attain the results at which I aimed. A company was formed, and ample funds seemed assured. This expedition was to be the big test, the real proof of the future possibilities of submarine photography.

Many anxious days and nights were devoted to planning everything to the most minute detail. I visited the Pennsylvania steel mills and arranged for the casting of my new deep-sea 'photosphere', which,

complete with its great glass windows, would weigh nearly four tons. Optical experts in Rochester accepted my specifications for lenses and film. Mercury vapour lighting engineers contracted to provide proper illumination by means of my new deep sea lamps.

With all equipment ready for shipment, and all business details arranged, I sailed for the port of Nassau in February of 1914. A shower of tropical

On the surface the parent ship. Stretching down from it, the Williamson submarine tube; at the end of it the photo sphere and the bank of underwater lights which made it possible to take the first undersea motion pictures

sunshine descended as the tender entered the harbour, and I blinked with amazement at the transparency of the water. 'That's it' I shouted involuntarily, to assure myself that it was true. If anyone heard me, he could not know of the months of anxiety behind my expression of joy. I was nearing my goal. After a month in Nassau, my work vessel was ready. Rapidly the apparatus was assembled. The massive undersea chamber slipped downward through the well into the sea. We were ready for our submarine adventure....

BENEATH TROPIC SEAS

With a whirr of gears, our tunnel of steel slid gently into the sea. Like a mammoth antenna, the flexible tube felt its way giving and taking to the currents, curving to their flow, until five fathoms of its length had been lowered through the open well in the bottom of our craft. The chamber was close to the bottom. The hour of our supreme test had arrived. With a shout of elation I descended into the tube,

The steel photo sphere designed by J. E. Williamson

followed by the others. Reaching the photosphere I stood spellbound at the sight which greeted me. Could this be real, or was I dreaming? Nothing I had ever imagined had equalled this. It was more than I had dared hope for. Down from above through the crystal clear waters streamed the bright sunlight, which, striking the white marl bottom, was reflected in a glittering, rippling plane of light. No artificial illumination was needed. We couldn't fail in this light. The camera would tell the story.

For our test we had several skilful diving boys already enrolled as members of our crew. Shillings and quarter-dollars were piled on deck and eagerly the black boys pressed forward listening to my instructions. All was ready. Descending into the camera chamber where the movie apparatus was loaded and focused I gave the signal, 'Go'. Down through the water dropped the coins, slowly, gently, catching the glint of the sun first on one side and then on the other as they descended. And down after them came

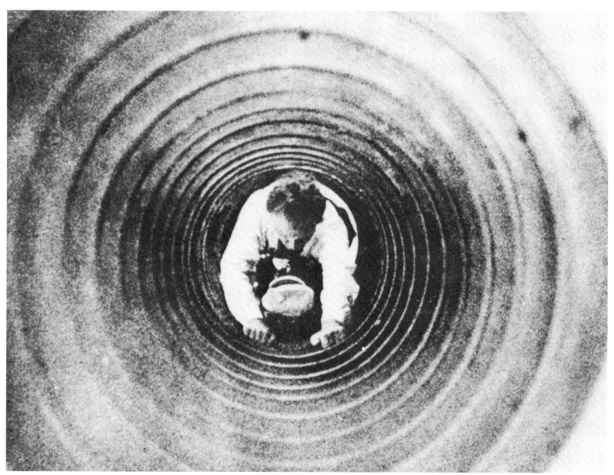

J. E. Williamson descending the submarine tube into the photo sphere

the boys, flashing downward with long swift strokes, white-soled feet kicking, and leaving a trail of silvery bubbles in their wake. And what action! Before the window of our photosphere, under the eye of the clicking camera, they fought and struggled. They searched in the soft white marl for lost coins and looked like blue ghosts in the cloud of white ooze stirred up by their efforts. Again and again they dived into our field of vision, until the supply of coins was exhausted. But it was enough: we had shot the first motion pictures ever taken under the sea. I was supremely, crazily happy, for I was as certain as I had ever been of anything that the film had recorded every detail, that motion pictures beneath the sea were not only possible, but an accomplished fact.

We had pitched our dark-room in an old stone building buried in a cluster of coco-nut trees and fragrant flowers that opened at night. The darker the night the darker the room inside, for through chinks in the crumbling building could be seen the twinkling heavens above; here in this ancient structure haunted by ghosts of a romantic past, we would

A shoal of fish, sergeant majors, convict fish, and schoolmasters parade before the magic window of the Williamson photo sphere

know our future. I helped with the ice and brought water from an aged well. My mind was in a jumble, and I felt like a prisoner who awaits the verdict of the jury. I kept as close as possible to the tanks and to the dark-room. Dead silence. Then grunts in the tank-room gave way to sounds which were more encouraging.

I knew when the singing commenced it was time to go in, and I stole through the curtained opening with that wonderful feeling of exhilaration that comes from knowing that a victory has been won. It was

there in that strip of film. In the tiny frames no larger than a row of postage stamps were the negatives, the first undersea motion pictures in the world.

Too excited to sleep, too filled with emotion to dream of retiring, I wandered to the edge of the sea that stretched black and mysterious, reflecting like a mirror the brilliant stars of the tropical sky above. Not until the eastern sky paled with the coming of dawn did I seek our sleeping quarters.

The following week was one of hectic work. Buoyantly confident, now that our first tests had

J. E. Williamson and his wife and baby daughter about to descend
into the photo sphere beneath the waves

proved so successful, we rushed blindly ahead and sailed forth into the open sea. Deeper and deeper we lowered the photosphere at the end of its flexible tube. But we were veritable tenderfeet at this game. We were in an unknown realm dealing with strange forces and we had much to learn. We discovered this one day when we lowered our apparatus among the great coral reefs. Breathless with wonder at the weird beauty of the undersea life unfolding in colourful panorama before us, we were gazing entranced when, like a flock of frightened birds, a school of fish dashed past our window. The next instant the great steel photosphere tipped and swayed as we were caught in an undersea current. With a sickening, terrifying crash we were dashed against a great dome-shaped mass of coral. The flexible tube bent and, together with everything movable, we were tumbled head over heels. Yet in the terror and excitement of that moment my mind fastened upon one vital thing – the big glass window. If that went, if it were broken or even cracked, my experiments under the ocean would be over. Fate was kind to us. By pure luck, or through the intervention of Providence, the glass did not strike the coral and the next moment we had dragged over the reef and once more were poised upright and safe in open water beyond the dangerous mass. The ingenious bending of the tube had saved us.

Both day and night work was the order. Then, as the culmination of that week of labour, my brother, clad in a diving suit, dropped to the sea's floor among the coral reefs where we had discovered the wreck of some long-forgotten ship. In ghostly pantomime he moved about the ribs and backbone of the ancient hulk, while a stream of air bubbles rushed from the helmet to the surface far above. Here was a thrill. Among the rotted timbers the outlines of corroded cannon could be seen. And though no bars of bullion or silver coins rewarded his search, yet we obtained our treasure – treasure more precious to us than doubloons and plate – the recorded film of an actual treasure hunt at the bottom of the sea.

A DUEL WITH A MAN-EATER

Before starting on the expedition, I had, in an optimistic moment, assured our financial backers that our undersea movies would include a shark fight – an actual combat between a man and a savage tiger of the sea. I had not for a moment forgotten that promise. In fact, I was constantly reminded of it as sharks flirted about our undersea chamber day and night. A horse for bait was the positive decree of the natives; a horse we must have to obtain results. We sent men ashore to round up some decrepit beast whose days were numbered anyway. The search proved futile. We advertised, but received no answer. We began to feel a great deal of sympathy for the king who shouted, 'A horse a horse my kingdom for a horse'. We felt the same way.

Finally, when we had just about given up hope, we located a man who owned an old horse that was lame and had been condemned to be shot. Immediately we negotiated for the carcass. The owner was to make delivery the next morning in our yard at the waterfront. Came the dawn. Came the man, and worst of all, came the horse. The reports of his expected demise, like Mark Twain's death, had been grossly exaggerated. No animal could be shot, it appeared, without an official British Government permit. We were in a real dilemma. Suddenly there came the flash of spiked helmets in the sun, accompanied by the military tramp of feet, and swinging into our yard came a guard of the Bahamas police in the charge of an officer. They came to a halt near the horse, which was thoroughly examined and found lame. With great formality the officer read aloud to the horse the permit. A soldier handed him a pneumatic gun. With neither a murmur nor a sigh our horse sat down, then lay down, its troubles definitely over.

In the business of shark fighting, tense moments were to come. A crew of men had been detailed to look after our bait, which was suspended from a boom and allowed to sink down into the sea for a safe distance. First came two grey monsters, wary, circling about, baleful eyes alert, grinning teeth bared. But they were suspicious. Suddenly turning, they sped away. Soon others appeared, wrinkling their blunt snouts and rolling their eyes upward as they caught the scent of blood. They also retreated. Again and again this was repeated, but each time the sharks approached they were in greater numbers and each time they were bolder, hungrier, and more anxious to hurl themselves blindly at the tempting bait floating above our photosphere. Presently with a rush, one great monster flashed upward with open jaws. The men on the deck were ready for just such an emergency. Quickly they raised the boom, lifting the carcass clear of the water. Chagrined, the shark slunk back, but he lurked nearby, and when the bait was lowered again, he and his companions made a concerted rush. This time the men were not quick enough. The sharks threw themselves upon the meat, tearing at it, shaking it as a terrier shakes a rat, gulping down great mouthfuls. Once they had tasted it, they forgot all caution, all suspicion. They had but one urge, and when the bait was lifted and they were baffled, they became obsessed with a maniacal fury and snapped and tore blindly at one another. Good, the madder they became, the better for us, the more savage would they appear in our picture, and the more thrilling would be the final scene of battle.

The human shark fighters appeared quite unconcerned about the ravenous beasts. While the sharks were being goaded into a frenzy, their human antagonists were rubbing oil into their black skins, the younger diving boys gazing at them in awe and admiration. Time for action had come. Summoning one of them, I told him all was ready, to choose his moment and go for it. Pointing down through the clear water, I warned him to be sure and stage his duel in front of the window or all our work would be lost. I explained that he must start when his intended victim was in position. It was not a simple matter even for a person who understood the limitation of our camera movements within the photosphere, and I could see that such details meant little to this native, who, never in his life, had even seen a motion picture.

Sharks were now cruising about: the time had come. Grasping his long-bladed knife in his teeth, he dived. We watched tense, thrilled, excited. Like a skilled matador in the bull-ring, the man was placing himself in position to strike home a death blow, and, like a wary bull, the shark was doing the same. They circled about, moving quickly first one way and then another. A moment more and both antagonists had swung far out of the range of the camera. We yelled. We shouted. It did no good. He could not hear us, and even if he could, it would not have helped matters. It was too late for him to change his tactics. The position of the shark controlled matters down there. Hauling wildly at the gear, sweating, shouting, our crew fought madly to swing the vessel and bring the photosphere into position. But affairs moved swiftly. With a sudden forward dash, the diver drove his knife up to the hilt into his enemy. It was a wonderful and spectacular feat, but completely lost to the camera. The diver bobbed up, grinning and triumphant. He danced on deck and boasted of his prowess. He had killed a shark, and he went below well satisfied with his day's work. He was through. Failure, utter failure after all our preparations and trouble. We seemed to have reached the end of our resources. A shark fight without a fighter was impossible, and we had no fighter. Utterly depressed and discouraged, I seated myself on the capstan. I had given my word that we would film a shark fight and we had failed. We had shot nearly two miles of film and all we needed were a few yards more, a few yards that might mean overwhelming success. They would be the punch we needed to put the whole thing over.

Suddenly I was inspired. I would get that picture. I would fight the shark myself. I pulled off my clothing, cut short the legs of my thin trousers, and borrowed a long-bladed native shark knife. If a Bahaman negro could fight a shark, I could. I was as good a swimmer

*An amazing photograph of a native West Indian diver
in the act of knifing a shark*

as any of the men, I was stronger and more physically fit than any of the natives. Moreover, I had watched every movement, every feint, every turn and twist of the diver who had killed the shark. Possibly I was over-confident. But by watching sharks in their natural habitat, under all sorts of conditions, I had acquired a deep knowledge of their ways and motions. Walking aft, I called all hands on deck and told them of my decision. Eyes rolled. Mouths opened in amazement. No one had ever heard of a white man attempting the feat. I was going to my death, they felt certain. But they rubbed me down with their oil, which they. declared was a secret compound. Perhaps it was, for I have never smelled

anything to equal it. Below in the watery arena I could count the sharks – twelve great brutes. If only one more would arrive. If only they would total my lucky number – thirteen.

Down through the water I plunged and swam. With a sweep of an arm, I veered to one side and the next instant was beneath the shark. What a monster he was. But I had no time to dwell on this, no time to repent of my hare-brained adventure. It was too late for retreat, for with a flirt of his tail the shark had turned and was dashing open-mouthed at me. Now the great grey body was almost upon me. I remembered the native diver's trick. Veering aside, I grasped the monster's fin, felt my hand close upon it. With a twist, I was under the livid white belly at the spot I was trying to reach. With all my strength I struck. A quivering thrill raced up my arm as I felt the blade bury itself to the hilt in the flesh, and the next moment I was swung right and left by a lashing body. Then a blur, confusion – chaos. I believed I was swimming, desperately, striving madly to reach the surface, but I could not be sure. Everything seemed hazy, indistinct. Hands slapping my back brought me back to reality with a jerk. Somehow I had managed to reach the deck. Everyone was shouting and congratulating me. I had killed a shark.

A week later we boarded the steamer for New York, our precious film guarded like a chest of gold. There was much to be done before the results of our expedition could be shown to the world. Five weeks in the cutting room and laboratory found us with a complete celluloid ribbon, 6,000 feet long. Six reels of film representing all our hopes and ambitions: a tiny package a foot square.

With this box of treasure we boarded the train for Washington DC, where the Smithsonian Institute was to give the initial exhibition of our film. Newspapers had announced the event and the imagination of the public had been aroused. The demand for admission had been unprecedented, overwhelming the officials of the Institute. Scientists and members filled the huge auditorium at the scheduled four o'clock showing, and they liked it. But it was the verdict of the amusement-seeking public upon which we depended for financial success. Our pictures had no story, no plot. They had to be presented as a film feature, solely on their own merits, as a record of our undersea expedition. As such they must succeed or fail. A noted and experienced showman declared that the pictures would not go over. Film features were built about a love theme and sex. The people had come to expect a story, heart interest with every reel of film.

Well, there was but one way to prove whether he was right or wrong – to show the films. We would open on Broadway, bored, thrill-weary, sophisticated Broadway, the crucible of all shows. We would occupy a new theatre, with our undersea pictures as the sole attraction. The show was a hit. Critics exploded with superlatives of praise. 'Amazing. Thrilling. Something entirely new. Something never before viewed by mankind.' We had brought the bottom of the sea to Broadway and Broadway liked it. After taking Gotham by storm our feature ran for seven months in Chicago. London was the next citadel to fall. And so around the world. If there was nothing new under the sun, the 'Williamson Submarine Expedition' had proved that there was something new to be seen under the sea.

MAKING JULES VERNE'S DREAM COME TRUE

As surely as undersea movies followed my first still photographs, we were destined to film Jules Verne's world-famous story, *Twenty Thousand Leagues Under the Sea*. This golden opportunity presented itself immediately after I had startled the world with the magic of motion pictures from the bottom of the sea. You will have to get back to Broadway – the Broadway of 1915 – to feel the public enthusiasm that was carrying us along to success in the rising industry of movie pictures. Growing with us was something of even greater moment – the distant rumblings of the World War. The United States was two years away from it, yet close enough for the public to begin to sense the terrible menace of one of the outstanding features of the war, the deadly submarine. Death was stalking beneath the sea; striking from the dark. Stark tragedy was being enacted thousands of miles away, yet close enough to fire the imagination of the most blasé Broadwayite. Doubly blessed, we were right on Broadway, with 'The Williamson Submarine Expedition' which, while it gave only a peep into the wonders and mysteries of the deep, was a revelation and sensational entertainment.

With the Jules Verne story, dominated by the fascinating Captain Nemo, we could go on into the depths – to the bottom of the ocean. It was great to be in on such a boom, to be able to give the public what it wanted, a real photoplay, a human drama, different from our current picture which had no plot, no story – just the drift of a unique expedition. Now we could play human emotions against the throbbing background of the mysterious undersea world. To vindicate Verne, the dreamer, was my problem as I set out to supervise the production of the picture – to make Jules Verne's dream come true.

But where were the unique and extraordinary props? For our venture we needed a submarine to represent the Nautilus, a ship for the Abraham Lincoln, a yacht to be torpedoed, and of vital importance, diving suits which would enable men to wander over the sea floor without life-lines, air-tubes or other connection with the surface. I had scarcely started my search when I learned from a chance-met veteran diver that suits such as I needed were being manufactured in England. Within two days fifteen suits had been ordered and, with the co-operation of the Navy Department, I had engaged a number of the best divers in the United States to sail with me for the Bahama Islands within a month. At last, after an almost endless search, I found an old brig which, with alterations, might serve as the Abraham Lincoln. By sheer good luck, also, I came upon a long-unused yacht that might have been a sister ship of the vessel we needed. Fortune seemed to smile again. I was as tickled as a cat with two tails. With the divers, the frigate and the yacht in readiness, we were all ready to sail for the Bahamas.

There was still the biggest problem of all – that of the submarine. There was only one way to get the craft, and that was to build it. Here my training in marine engineering would serve me well, and soon the submarine was rapidly taking form and substance. When completed she was well over a hundred feet in length, and she can best be described by quoting from Jules Verne's account of the Nautilus. 'It was an elongated cylinder with conical ends, very like a cigar in shape . . . with iron plates slightly over-laying each other, resembling the shells which close the bodies of large terrestrial reptiles. . . . The steel plates were held together by thousands of rivets. . . .' Unlike Captain Nemo's Nautilus, my submarine could be controlled entirely by one man. By filling tanks with water it could be submerged. By emptying them it could be raised to the surface, and it could be steered to port or starboard or manoeuvred generally by the single operator. Moreover, in addition to the air lock in which Captain Nemo and his men left the Nautilus to wander upon the floor of the ocean, my Nautilus was equipped with torpedo tubes.

THE FIRST FILM DRAMA BENEATH THE SEA

At last all seemed ready. We could now begin the actual filming of Jules Verne's marvellous tale. Actually there was but one serious trouble, and that sprang from the chemicals used in our new self-contained diving suits. As we progressed with our undersea work, I discovered that the divers, stimulated by the effects of the chemicals they breathed, felt dreamily happy after being down three or four hours, and often, after playing their parts in a scene, they would wander away on excursions of their own, exploring coral caves or picking sea anemones and would be missing when we required them for the next scene. It was a curious experience to have these hardened veterans in this serious work go off picking flowers like children. It was also dangerous. The chemical used, oxylithe, when exhausted affects the diver's brain like alcohol and constant care must be taken that the charges are renewed promptly every hour.

On one occasion, working overtime in an emergency we came uncomfortably close to tragedy.

The divers had emerged from the air-lock of the Nautilus to the sea-floor, and had been working for a long time in a particularly thrilling scene. As they prepared to re-enter the submarine, they suddenly fell upon one another like maniacs, fighting desperately. Struggling, utterly crazed by the exhausted chemical, one of the men was caught in the current, swept off his feet, and knocking a valve which inflated his suit, was thrashing aimlessly towards the surface. Helpless, entirely out of his mind, I fear to think of the consequences had it not been for Biggie, a seven-foot giant and one of my native Bahamas crew, who reached down from our diving boat as the diver swept by, and grabbing him with one hand he landed him weights and all right on to our deck. Had his rescue been delayed a moment longer he might have submerged again and been lost. Even as it was the diver's face was horribly black. He was foaming at the mouth. It took five men to hold him down as he fought like a demon, before slowly returning to normal.

Day by day, week by week, the reels of the exposed film increased. Thousands of feet had been shot.

A diver fends off the attack of a moray eel

MISHAPS AND ADVENTURES

Only two really big scenes remained to be filmed; the torpedoing of the yacht, and finally, the undersea battle with an octopus. This battle would be truly a daring undertaking, and, if anything went wrong, it might mean an 'undertaking' in more ways than one.

However, the giant creature was yet to be located, so while the search continued I decided that next in order was the sinking of the yacht. There would be no doubt as to the full destruction of the craft. We were going to photograph the explosion as the torpedo from the Nautilus struck her. When the yacht sailed to her doom, she would carry a cargo of enough dynamite, black powder and petrol to blow up a battleship. Everything must go like clockwork, for this was a scene that could not be retaken. We had one chance and only one, to get a successful picture. More than £5,000 was to go up in flames and smoke. We couldn't afford to fail. Every detail, every act, every movement of every participant, whether actor or crew member, must be timed to a split second.

The plan was as follows. The yacht was to be placed near some rocks that jutted out of the ocean, and on which the camera men were to be stationed. At a given signal, which was to be two pistol shots, the men on board the yacht were to touch off the time fuse on the explosives, and dash away to safety in their motor-boats, while the Nautilus was to run into the scene in order to save the hero and heroine, who were to leap from the doomed yacht into the sea, and be picked up by Captain Nemo and his crew. Of course, everybody and his neighbour's wife in the port of Nassau had heard of the spectacle about to be staged, and hundreds of pleasure craft had put to sea that day, and gathered about us at a safe distance, that is, as close as possible without being in the actual scene itself. Steaming into the foreground was the Governor's launch, with His Excellency, his wife and a party on board, the Governor having accepted our invitation to be present on this occasion. It looked like a gala day. Everything was going along splendidly.

Suddenly from the direction of the rocks came the report of a pistol shot. I sprang to my feet. It could not be the pre-arranged signal – the allotted moment had not arrived. The Nautilus was far from the yacht, while the Governor's launch was within a few dozen yards of it. But the men who were to touch off the explosives had been warned to act on the instant. At the crack of the pistol, they leaped to their task, never waiting for the second shot, and by the time I reached the deck they were dashing away in their motor-boat. The explosion was coming. I held my breath. The Governor of the Bahamas was well within the danger zone. He was standing there with his wife and party on the bridge of his launch, looking at the yacht, not knowing it would explode in their faces at any moment; and to add to my horror the launch, Governor and all, must surely be in the picture. A volcano seemed to burst into eruption. Flames, smoke, shattered planking and timbers were flung high in the air. Debris showered about the Governor's vessel.

Then I jumped into action. Somebody had made a mistake, but it was too late to do anything about it. Out there on the water, £5,000 worth of yacht was going up in fire and smoke. Her bow was sticking up in the air – in a moment she would sink. I headed the Nautilus into the scene towards the blazing remains of the yacht. Slowly we neared the projecting bow. Every effort was made to clear it, but the current was sweeping us so close that the actors on the deck of the Nautilus could have reached out and touched the bow of the sinking yacht with their hands. I was just below them in the open hatch, safely out of the range of the grinding cameras.

The scene on the Nautilus was impressive, regardless of the catastrophe. Captain Nemo stood erect, formidable, arms folded across his chest, his revenge now complete. Tears streamed down the heroine's face as she went through the pantomime of thanking Captain Nemo for her rescue, but I could see from her trembling that her tears were not all acting. The hero, fully alive to the tenseness of the moment, was manfully acting his part. As far as the camera was concerned, this part of the scene was perfect, for, just as we passed the yacht, she slipped back into the sea, plunging to the green depths below. It was over. There were cheers from the spectators. Their Governor was safe. Although timbers flew all about his party no one was injured. Again the onlookers cheered and cheered. Then boats scattered in every direction, homeward bound, or to fishing grounds or bathing beaches. It had been a great show. Soon the last of the pleasure craft disappeared into the distance.

A starlit night settled down on us before we had assembled our men and equipment and started our trek back to the harbour at Nassau eight miles away. Exhausted, utterly discouraged, it was all painfully clear to me now. The end of the scene could be used, even as it went off loaded with death; but the beginning, the explosion on the yacht, a six-foot flash costing £1,000 a foot, would be a total waste if the Governor's launch appeared in the scene. And all because a fool assistant, wishing to make sure that the pistol was in working order, had fired a shot to test it. And now the suspense. We would not dare develop this precious strip of film in the tropical heat of our testing laboratory at Nassau, served only by rainwater from the housetops. We must wait for the laboratories in New York to give us the result of the development. That was all that could be done about it. Wait. The camera men had been questioned. They did not know. Flying splinters from the explosion had reached them on the island. In the excitement of the moment, and not looking for the launch to be in the picture, they could not be sure about it. It might be in the picture – and it might not. All this uncertainty only added to the agony of suspense, growing through the days of waiting until the cable arrived from New York. It read, 'Launch not in picture'. The scene was a knock-out. It was perfect.

At last the great day arrived for the battle with the giant octopus, a natural climax to our thrilling undersea adventure. I knew where my octopus was lurking. The stage was set. One of my most daring divers would take the part of Captain Nemo. I was confident he would go through with the scene successfully, but I was not so sure of the native diver who was to take the part of the pearl fisher. To assure realism I had had this man agree to play the part, dive in and gather his pearls, without his knowing exactly what was going to happen to him. He knew that something unusual was up when he saw several armoured divers sink silently down into the sea, just outside the camera range. However, the native had sublime confidence in me, and the promise of a big bonus if he made good.

With the octopus, the pearl diver, and Captain Nemo all at hand, we were ready to go. We were prepared to undertake the filming of the most astounding and extraordinary scene ever attempted. I could not but admire the daring of the native who was to act the part of the pearl fisher as I signalled him to stand by for his plunge into the water: a human bait for the monster octopus. Surrounded by a frame of gleaming silver bubbles, the native came plunging into view. And then a shudder ran through me. I knew what to expect, but the actual sight of that great pulpy body, those great staring eyes, those snake-like sucker-armed tentacles, sent a chill of horror down my spine. The giant cuttle-fish glided with sinuous motion from its lair, a thing to inspire terror in the stoutest heart. The native saw it. He turned – struck out for the surface. Too late. Like a striking serpent, one great writhing tentacle shot out and threw a coil about the hapless swimmer. Frantically he struggled, but the sinuous arm of the octopus drew him down inexorably. Here was stark realism. All the while the clicking of the camera told me that not one detail of the gruesome scene was being missed. How much longer could the native struggle there beneath the sea?

'Captain Nemo's' real-life battle with the octopus

Into the field of vision came the grotesque figure of the helmeted diver, the gallant Captain Nemo. Now he was beside the native who was struggling in the clutches of the squirming python-like tentacle. A flash of his broad-bladed axe – the tentacle fell – and the struggling native shot to the surface, gasping for breath but saved. A great cloud of ink gushed from the octopus, blackening the sea about the wounded monster, obscuring the courageous Captain Nemo, and through the murky screen I caught glimpses of the writhing, twisting tentacles, flashes of the axe, and the struggling, grotesque form. Elated, I yelled with joy. Suddenly a current swept the inky veil aside. With his body wrapped about by the clinging tentacles, Nemo was battling furiously, while beyond him, unspeakably horrid and menacing, were the great round staring eyes, the huge pinkish body. But one by one the gripping tentacles were relaxing their hold. The creature seemed ready to abandon the struggle. Another cloud of ink enshrouded the scene, and when the water cleared, Nemo was moving toward us, axe in hand. The master scene was over.

With this epic battle on the ocean's floor filmed my undersea work on *Twenty Thousand Leagues Under the Sea* was complete. In the opinion of a famous newspaper critic, 'If the rest of the picture were discarded, the undersea scenes alone would be worth three times the price of admission'. It seemed that we had timed our entrance into the picture-show world just right, for by the strangest coincidence, the picture opened the same day that a German U-boat suddenly appeared on the coast of the United States, electrifying the nation and monopolizing the headlines with the news that the elusive U-boat had slipped through all blockades, crossed the Atlantic Ocean, and had torpedoed and sunk half a dozen British ships just outside New York. Later the submarine slipped safely back to Germany. To quote one of the leading Chicago papers, 'If the Kaiser had been its press agent, *Twenty Thousand Leagues Under the Sea* could not have been timed to better advantage'.

EPILOGUE

In the years that followed the success of *Twenty Thousand Leagues*, Williamson shot a string of feature films and a number of early scientific submarine films – the first under-water documentaries. In fact he honey-mooned afloat in the Bahamas, and next year brought his new wife – and even newer daughter – back on a major scientific assignment for the Field Museum of Chicago, to bring back 'Seven Habitat Groups of Bahaman Fishes' for the 'Hall of the Ocean Floor'; his wife helpfully becoming the world's first submarine typist, as she kept production notes.

Yet in many respects Williamson was a feature director by nature, and features provided his biggest excitement – and disappointments. In particular there was the 'master film' of the re-make of *Twenty Thousand Leagues* some ten years later – all in colour, and on almost the first million-dollar budget. But what was planned as a 'great super spectacle' faded into 'a hushed and silent spectre' – for the 'talkies' had arrived.

For excitement and satisfaction, Williamson probably got most from his own films. A typical Williamson moment came in *Girl of the Sea*, and let the director himself have the last word.

'Another time, the unforeseen gave me some nerve-torturing moments that have never been equalled during my twenty years of adventures beneath the sea. I was directing the undersea scenes of another of my own film productions, *Girl of the Sea*. Its story was my own. I had an excellent diver who doubled for the hero, and seated in the chamber of my photosphere with my camera man cranking beside me, I looked out at this diver at work among the ruins of a gruesome and rotting old vessel on the floor of the sea. There, on the slimy floor, was a human skeleton. Projecting from between the ribs was the handle of a murderous knife. Upon one bony finger was a curious antique ring. The entire plot of the story hinged upon

71

the diver's recovery of the ring and the knife. But it seemed difficult for this man, locked in a diving suit, to put into convincing action the intimate details of the scene. Again and again the action was repeated and each time it was worse than before.

At last, I decided to do the close-ups myself. Hurrying to the surface, I seized upon the first suit at hand, an old one, long unused. Dropping into the sea, I changed places with the diver. Cautiously I withdrew the knife, and moving closer, I lifted the skeleton hand to remove the ring from the dead man's finger.

At this tense moment inside my copper helmet I felt something moving. Something was crawling — creeping through my hair . . . moving with pin-pointed feet down my forehead. Now the fearsome thing was crawling down my nose, I could see it. My hair seemed to stand on end. The thing was a scorpion. I controlled a desire to dash my head against the inside of the helmet and try to crush the venomous creature. But I knew that at the slightest movement it might bury its poisonous sting in my flesh — even in my eye. No, I must be cool, must control myself. . . . With

Mrs Williamson takes notes during a scientific voyage — the first underwater secretary

unspeakable relief I felt the creature crawl back into my hair. And all this time, while my mind was numb with dread of the scorpion imprisoned in my helmet, I was going through with my part, acting out the scene, while the cameras clicked away and the operators marvelled at the vivid realism of my acting, little dreaming that it was a scorpion in my helmet that was filling me with the emotions I was exhibiting.

When at last the helmet was lifted and I told my story, I was greeted with questioning looks from my men. There was no sign of a scorpion anywhere. Nothing, however, would convince me that this awful creature had been a figment of an overwrought mind. I examined the interior of the helmet. Nothing there. Then I had a sudden inspiration. From the air-tube at the back of the helmet several flat channels led in various directions, to distribute the air throughout the helmet. And when a blast of air was forced through these channels, out came the scorpion. . . .'

Across Greenland

Greenland: the largest island in the world, and in 1930 still largely unknown, covered by a vast ice-sheet from which ancient glaciers that date back to the last ice-age dribbled down to the coast. Meteorologically it was a staging-post for the depressions and storms which drifted down from the Arctic, and so emperilled the pioneer aviators as they attempted to hedge-hop the North Atlantic from Prestwick in Scotland via Gander in Newfoundland, and so on to the North American continent. To any

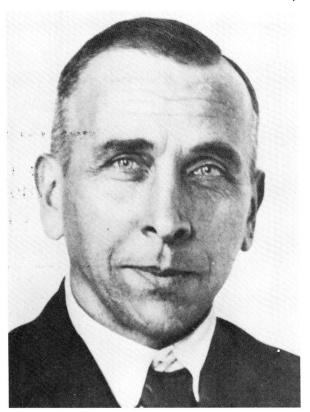

Dr Alfred Wegener, leader of the German Greenland expedition

scientist/explorer there was a wealth of knowledge just waiting to be gathered; to one who had once fallen under its frozen spell, a place of enchantment, to be returned to, whatever the cost. Such a man was Dr Alfred Wegener; Professor of Geophysics and Meteorology at the University of Graz in Germany, a specialist in glaciology and a leading scientist of his day. His achievements range from being a member of the Danish Greenland Expedition of 1906–07, to publishing the Displacement of Continents Theory in 1912.

And in 1928, Greenland again – the start of Wegener's last expedition. His widow, Else Wegener, describes how it all began:

> We had almost settled down to a life of middle-class comfort in the beautiful city of Graz. My husband lived for his scientific work. On Sundays, we went on what he called 'lowland tours' with the children in the delightful surroundings of Graz, in autumn 'highland tours' in the Alps, in winter ski-ing expeditions. It seemed as if this would go on indefinitely. Forgotten were the hardships of the crossing of Greenland, which had left a deep impression on those at home also, for we had been without news for a whole year.
>
> Then at Easter, 1928 we had a visit from Professor Meinardus of Gottingen. It was only a short visit in passing, merely to find out whether Alfred Wegener would act as leader of a small summer expedition to Greenland . . . Greenland. Old plans were revived. . . .

The plans were bold and ambitious: a year-long study of the ice-cap and meteorology of Greenland. Three major Observation Stations were to be set up on the inland ice plateau – one on the Eastern edge, one on the Western, and one right in the frozen heart –

'Eismitte' – to carry out observations of all kinds. The thickness of the ice was to be measured with dynamite and echo-recorders: the atmosphere to be investigated with weather balloons and giant kites.

Altogether the expedition would number twenty people: Glaciologists, meteorologists, geologists, zoologists, surveyors and explosives experts to blast the ice. Pony handlers were to be brought to lead the

Icelandic pack ponies, aeronautical engineers to look after the propeller-driven motor sledges, of which Wegener had such high hopes.

By the spring of 1930 Wegener and all his colleagues, together with over one hundred tons of stores and scientific equipment, were assembled in Denmark, and ready to start on what was to be Wegener's last great expedition.

CHRONOLOGICAL SUMMARY

1 April 1930 Expedition sails from Copenhagen in the *Disko*.

15 April Arrival at Holstensborg.

7 May Ice blocks Kamarujuk Fiord.

17 June Expedition lands at head of Kamarujuk Fiord, six weeks late.

17 June–12 November Transport work goes on up glacier.

30 July Georgi, Weiken, and Greenlanders reach 250-mile point and establish Eismitte. First sledge journey.

6 August Start of second sledge journey to Eismitte.

29 August Start of third sledge journey to Eismitte.

17 September Motor-sledges start for Eismitte.

21 September Start of fourth sledge journey to Eismitte (Wegener, Loewe, and Greenlanders). They meet third party returning.

23 September Motor-sledge party turn back from 125-mile point.

24 September Wegener and Loewe meet motor-sledge party.

29 September Nine Greenlanders turn back from thirty-eight-and-a-half-mile point, with letters from Wegener.

5 October Georgi and Sorge move into underground cave at Eismitte.

7 October Three Greenlanders turn back from ninety-four-mile point, with letter from Wegener asking Weiken to send out a relief party; Wegener, Loewe, and Rasmus Villumsen go on.

Map showing the eastern station, the western station and the Eismitte station in the heart of the ice cap

27 October   Georgi and Sorge decide to winter at Eismitte.

30 October   Wegener, Loewe, and Rasmus reach Eismitte.

1 November   Wegener and Rasmus leave Eismitte for coast.

10 November   Weiken, Kraus, and two Greenlanders start on relief journey.

7 December   Relief party turn back.

23 April   Weiken and Greenlanders start for Eismitte.

7 May   Sledge parties reach Eismitte.

12 May   Dog-sledge party find Wegener's body 118 miles inland.

5–24 June   Sorge searches for body of Rasmus, in vain.

June and July   Measurements of thickness of ice thirty-seven miles inland.

24 July–6 August   Sorge measures thickness of ice at Eismitte.

7 August   Eismitte abandoned.

29 August   Georgi and Sorge leave for home (reach Copenhagen 23 September).

THE GERMAN SCIENTIFIC EXPEDITION TO GREENLAND, 1930–31, by Dr Alfred Wegener, Dr Ernst Sorge and Dr Karl Weiken

THE VOYAGE TO GREENLAND AND THE TIME OF WAITING AT UVKUSIGSAT
(From Alfred Wegener's Diary)

1 April 1930. On board the *Disko*. Sailed from Copenhagen at 10 o'clock this morning. Farewells and waving of handkerchiefs – now the link with home is broken and the expedition begins.

8 April. Reykjavik. We have just taken our twenty-five ponies on board. They are stoutly built and look just 'sweet'. Hope they will stand the sea passage well. . . . During the night the *Disko* was labouring so heavily that we were shipping heavy seas every minute. At 9 o'clock I went down to see the ponies. One cannot reach them without risking a soaking. All the ponies were in good form. They have already learned to stand firm without stumbling, in spite of the rolling of the ship.

14 April. Glorious weather, no wind, calm sea; splendid for the ponies. I have just been down looking at them. They are in high spirits. We are near the coast of Greenland, a chain of snow-clad peaks. Cold.

(On reaching Greenland, Wegener planned to sail north, 300 miles up to the coast, and then up the Kamarujuk Fiord, which he hoped would be free of ice by now. The next days were therefore spent in transferring his one hundred tons of stores and equipment to the expedition ship proper, the *Gustav Holm*.)

25 April. The *Gustav Holm* is a regular explorer's ship, with thick ice-sheathing and crow's nest. True, she offers us very cramped quarters, but the main thing is, all our goods are on board. Drums of paraffin are below in the coal bunkers; the deck is jammed with petrol cans, over which one has to pick one's way. On top of these is a boat, in which more petrol cans are stored. The dynamite is amongst the ponies' hay, the boxes of detonators in one of the life-boats. The provisions are at the very bottom under the hay.

Now we are taking on deck-cargo only. The huge packing-cases containing the motor-sledges stand right and left of the main hatch. If they had been an inch broader or ten inches longer they would not have gone in. The ponies are on deck in the lee of the packing-cases. One would imagine our belongings had been made to fit the *Gustav Holm*. The sledge dogs stink like the plague and are very dirty. They belong to no less than eleven different owners: how we shall ever find out which is whose again heaven only knows. Probably in October we shall bring back all the wrong dogs. But what else can we do? In all I reckon we have at the moment 110 borrowed dogs and ten of our own, and we are to get back twenty-three which are merely being fed up into condition, so that our real total is 145 dogs available.

27 April. On board the *Gustav Holm*. We are very comfortable on board our ship in spite of the cramped quarters. Two of us are still sleeping on the floor of the saloon as there are not enough cabins to go round, but amongst the hay there are sleeping-places ad lib.

30 April. We have a d-d risky cargo on board. If fire breaks out we're done for; no hope of putting out petrol. The only consolation is that we shall have a very imposing and expensive cremation ceremony.

2 May. This evening we said good-bye: hope everything will go well.

4 May. Now the difficulties are beginning. Early this morning we came to the edge of the ice which is still lying in front of Umanak. An attempt was made to break the ice and get into the bay, but it failed. Yes, it cannot be denied that the second item of our programme, reaching Kamarujuk Fiord with the *Gustav Holm*, has not come off. Now we must make up by hard work for what fortune has denied us.

6 May. At the edge of the ice. Yesterday was an eventful day. After two vain attempts to blast the ice with dynamite we managed to make a sort of harbour by ramming the ice.

10 May. We have spent our first night on Greenland. Now a new phase of the expedition begins, the vexatious time of waiting. We must keep cool. The Greenlanders are of the opinion that if the weather continues cold the ice will probably go out in fourteen days' time; if it turns warm, in eight days. Let's hope it will be warm, then. Today there is still a cool breeze from the sea.

19 May. Tenth day of waiting. Weather bad; heavy snowfall, mountains all hidden in mist. The ice has not noticeably receded.

3 June. Twenty-fifth day of waiting. Weather gloomy and my mood ditto. The programme of the expedition is getting seriously endangered by the refusal of the ice to move. Time is slipping by.

13 June. Thirty-fifth day of waiting. Now, at midnight, the sun is beautifully warm, but it is a dead calm; no sign of the east wind which would drive all the ice out.

16 June. Thirty-eighth day of waiting. A little after 1 a.m. we were roused by the Greenlander on watch shouting, 'The ice is going out'. An immense mass of ice had begun to move. Now we are only separated from the open water by a strip of ice five or six hundred yards across, which is already broken up by a pressure lane. In the afternoon we made an attempt to get into the lane of open water by blasting on a large scale – eighteen simultaneous explosions of three and a quarter pounds each. But this was a fiasco. In the first place, it took a long time to lay all the cables, and then the charges did not go off. After we had worked like this from 6 p.m. to 5 a.m. the ice opened up of itself, not where we were, but farther south. All our work had been wasted; we might as well have lain down and slept. How indifferent Nature is to our puny achievements. Full steam ahead into the new lane. At 7 a.m. we dropped anchor in Kamarujuk Fiord. Hurrah: our thirty-eight days of waiting off Uvkusigsat are at an end.

TRANSPORT JOURNEYS

17 June. At last our 2,500 boxes, cases, and cans have been landed at the head of Kamarujuk Fiord. We really have a marvellous collection of stuff. Lissey has just reckoned up that we have no less than 2,500 packages, a figure which horrified everybody. But if we count each package as weighing eighty-eight lbs, that makes ninety-eight tons, exactly what we are supposed to have. The appearance of our baggage is certainly imposing; one might even say hopeless, if

we did not also have a considerable number of men and ponies to deal with it. But we shall easily be able to get it over the glacier. By late evening there was a place for everything – goods, ponies and men. We quickly gulped down our pemmican and climbed up to the moraine.

The sun had set behind the steep cliffs which rose precipitously for over 3,000 feet and hemmed in the fiord and glacier on either side. So far as we could see, the glacier was free of snow. As smooth as a looking-glass, and practically without crevasses, it stretched up in a gentle curve to about 1,150 feet above sea-level. The expanse of glacier was cut off by the cliff, nearly 1,000 feet high, formed by the ice-fall or 'break' in the glacier. We anxiously scanned the maze of crevasses, ridges and pinnacles. We shook our heads and strolled back to the big summer tent. Here a council of war was already in progress.

18 June. Everybody hard at work. The road-making party, reinforced by half a dozen Greenlanders, buckled on their crampons and went up the glacier. Long stretches must first be hacked out of smooth walls of ice. So we were soon standing in the ice-fall, the 'break' in a long row, swinging our picks and sending blocks and splinters flying. The crevasses were blocked up with powdered ice at convenient narrow places. A few days of this work and the transport journeys could begin.

Now things went ahead in earnest. We all became transport workers and slaved from sunset to sunrise – for we worked at night; during the day it was too hot for man and beast in the burning glare of the sun on the glacier. Nothing but transport, transport, and still more transport. Pack ponies, porters, pony sledges, dog sledges, and motor-boat were all in continuous use. 'Keep things moving' was the watchword. The distance between sea level and the inland plateau was 2,970 feet. We soon noticed that our glacier which originally had seemed so dead and derelict was alive, in fact much too lively for our liking. Day by day, as the sun rose higher in the heavens, the melting of the

ice increased. The surface streams cut deeper and deeper into the ice; the crevasses got wider and wider. New work turned up daily. The tracks hewn in the ice were obliterated as the ice melted and had to be hacked out again and again. Night after night the strings of ponies crossed the glacier, but the great heap of goods at Kamarujuk simply refused to get noticeably smaller. We had to do all this ourselves as the Greenlanders were no use with the ponies. They were afraid of the 'big dogs', as they called them. At the foot of the glacier we loaded up. Heavens, what a weight those provision boxes were. They were supposed to weigh ninety-nine pounds, but they really weighed a third as much again. We found this out only too well when we had to handle them on the steep glacier slope with crampons on.

Up above the motor-sledge crews are working like mad. They are pulling their cars out of the gully of a stream with a winch and wire rope. Kraus is at the winch with a crowd of Greenlanders and shouts orders to them, 'Spillemik Assut Assut Quick'. The Greenlanders go on winding imperturbably at their own rate. 'Unipok, Stop, you rascals.' Now, of course they go on winding as if possessed. We are ready to die laughing.

One pony needs new shoes, but will not let himself be shod. We have to tie his legs with cords, throw him and shackle him. He is very strong: in spite of the shackles we can scarcely hold him. When Vigfus bends down to knock off the old shoes, he gives a great jerk and hits Vigfus right in the face with his left hind foot. So it comes about that this morning the pony has four new shoes on his feet and Vigfus two teeth less in his mouth. With that our night's work is done.

So it went on day after day, week after week in never-ending monotony. By night we led the ponies over the glacier, by day we lay in the incubator-like heat of the tent, trying in vain to sleep. The Greenland summer is short but intense. We had to make the most of this season. The delay at Uvkusigsat had already made us horribly behind time. Not only had we to get everything on to the ice-cap, but we should have to make at least three sledge journeys in order to establish the Eismitte station in the middle of the icy waste 250 miles from the coast.

22 July. We have engaged fourteen more Greenlanders; we are now employing thirty-five in all. We must set our teeth and make transport journeys and yet more transport journeys if we are to get all the stuff up.

26 July. Up till now my gang of Greenlanders have worked splendidly. Yesterday we actually finished the long hairpin bend at the steepest part of the moraine in the forenoon. The lower half is 175 paces long, the upper 195. In the afternoon we advanced 160 feet on the ridge then doubled back 160 feet, then another bend and an advance of eighty feet. We were not out to beat records either, but to make sure that the track was broad and smooth. It is splendid to see how the Greenlanders work. European workers would not have done so much; they would not have moved so quickly. So we've won; the result far surpasses my

Hauling the aero sledges up the glacier with ponies and men

expectations, the Greenlanders are always cheerful and they are willing workers, so long as they look on the job as fun. Above all, they like good things to eat. 'Coffee-make' was always the first thing they asked for. This wish was easily granted; but what did they not need over and above? 'My kamiks (fur boots) are bad. My clothes are so thin and it's cold on the ice-cap. I haven't got a sleeping bag. I've lost my pipe. Haven't you got a pocket-knife for me? And my pants are worn out too.' Thus we were bombarded with requests.

5 August. It looks as if we are gradually being forced into a more and more awkward position. The short summer will soon be over and we have still a long way to go to the place we have fixed on for our winter hut. I am also seriously worried about the ice-cap station. The trouble is that the dogs alone cannot do it, so we must rely on the motor-sledges, which can carry any amount. We were late in reaching Kamarujuk; getting the stuff up on to the ice-cap has taken longer than we expected. Today I feel depressed and pessimistic. Success seems to be slipping from our grasp. But I am sure my plan of campaign is right. Ponies on the glacier, dog sledges and motor sledges across the ice-cap, that is the correct choice.

We begin a new epoch in Polar exploration. What we are doing here points the way at once for future Antarctic exploration. How wonderful that it should fall to us to make this pioneering step; nay, in view of the many air disasters which have occurred in Polar regions, I may say this redeeming step.

THE MOTOR-SLEDGES

Our two motor-sledges were specially built for the expedition by the Finnish State aeroplane factory at Helsingfors (where motor-sledges are used in the winter as a means of transport between the islands off the coast). They were streamlined, with a cabin for the driver and a roomy space for goods; the engine driving the propeller was at the rear. Although lightly constructed, they were extremely strong. They ran on four broad strong skids of hickory wood with rubber springs, two on the front axle, two on the rear. The front pair of skids could be moved just like the front wheels of a motor-car. Each sledge was driven by an air-cooled 110 h.p. Siemens Sh 12 aeroplane engine, and had a petrol tank holding sixty-three gallons.

We became navvies, spitting on our hands with a professional air, and laying about us with our ice-axes so that lumps of ice flew in all directions. Our blasting expert, Herdemerten, removed the worst obstacles very neatly with a few charges of explosive. Every time that we had prepared the 'road' for about 150 yards ahead, we pulled up the sledges and the engines one by one with a winch which we had anchored firmly in the ice. When the sledges and engines had been drawn up to the winch, another section of 'road' was made ready, the winch taken 150 yards farther on and firmly fixed in position and finally the sledges were pulled up to it again. It was wearisome work and took a long time. Never shall I forget our joyful yells when on 9 August we covered the last bit of the way.

Then came the great moment: the first trial of the engines. The whole lot of Greenlanders put in an appearance. They gaped curiously at the wonderful machine and kept getting in our way as we put the final touches. Meanwhile I put up a brief prayer that our engine would be so kind as to start up. We did not want to be put to shame in front of our Greenlander spectators, and those who are acquainted with aeroplane engines know that they are more uncertain in temperament than any old wife. It did start. Instantly the Greenlanders began running after their caps, which were blown off by the stream of air from the propellers, an effect for which they had not been prepared. For us the hum of the engines was heavenly music, for it meant the start of the motor-sledge journeys which we had been looking forward to for months.

We christened our sledges Schneespatz (Snow Bunting) and Eisbar (Polar Bear). We should really have had a bottle of champagne to smash against the sledges; in default of this, however, the christening ceremony was carried out with snowballs. The Greenlanders were speechless; they could not imagine a sledge running without dogs, and they still could not understand how we could get there merely by making a piece of wood on the sledge twirl in the air. Occasionally our engines were unkind enough to strike work. When it got too cold the petrol feeds and carburettor jets froze up. The engines also took a long time to start up. A leak in the petrol tank fifty-three miles out might easily have proved dangerous if we had not noticed it at once and made shift to mend it with our universal first-aid materials – string, insulating tape and wire.

5 September. We at last made our first long successful journey. The surface was so uneven that we could not keep up an average of more than eighteen and a half miles per hour; at higher speeds we should have risked smashing the skids. After a splendid run of three and a half hours, we got back to our tent at 'Start' that same evening. Our joy, however, was not to last long. That same evening a blizzard was again raging on the ice-cap; there were drifts higher than our heads and we could not see an arm's length ahead of us. All the same, we started the next day in hazy weather with about nine hundredweights of effective load, as well as provisions and a tent, in each sledge. We again had extreme difficulty in starting; the sledges stuck in the fresh snow as if they had roots. We were nearly driven to despair. With the engines running full speed we shook and pushed with levers, all four men at one sledge; but it took us hours to get it to move.

17 September. We have finally started for Eismitte. We had already taken on the greater part of the load and some cans of petrol to the 125-mile depot. After driving for five hours we reached the 125-mile depot – the half-way point – shortly before darkness fell.

Excellent progress. One more day like this, and we will reach Eismitte tomorrow night.

18 September. Early this morning when we were preparing to start at 6 a.m. we were met by thick mist and driving snow. We rushed to clear the sledges, which were half buried in snowdrifts. First we tried to start up Eisbar's engine. After a lot of trouble and spraying the inlets with considerable quantities of petrol ether we did manage to get it running. With the Schneespatz we had no luck. The engine simply would not budge. Neither petrol ether nor hot oil, neither kind words nor well-intentioned remarks in coarser language would induce it to start. For hours on end we tried turning the propeller, backwards and forwards, quickly and slowly; we examined the sparking-plugs; in short, we did everything that can be done to an aeroplane engine, with no result whatever. At last, after we had heated the engine for an hour and a half with our primus and soldering lamps, it gave in and started. We had barely started, however, when alas we found that once more we had counted our chickens before they were hatched. Owing to the recent heavy fall of snow and the head-wind, the heavily-laden sledges could make no progress. Although the engines were running at full power and the second man jumped out and pushed behind, we remained stuck. We now realised that it was hopeless to contend further against the powers of the winter which had suddenly set in. We must give in and resign ourselves to the fact that it was goodbye to motor-sledge journeys on the ice-cap this year.

It was an unspeakably heavy blow for us to have to turn back only one day's journey from our destination. So the motor sledges, on which so much depended, had failed. Meanwhile the last of the stores had been portaged up the glacier, and the expedition had set up its main Western Station, where scientists would spend the winter: and they had also succeeded in making three dog-sledge journeys into the centre of the great ice-plateau, and establishing EISMITTE, 'HEART OF THE ICE' camp, 250 miles inland, at

The aero sledge Eisbar (Ice-bear), helpless in a crevasse. It was the failure of the motor sledges which cost Dr Wegener his life

present manned by just two scientists, Dr Ernest Sorge, glaciologist, and Dr Johanns Georgi, the meteorologist in charge of Eismette.

(The situation now at the beginning of September – in fact before the motor-sledges had made their unsuccessful attempt – was that more food and paraffin must be got to Eismitte if the two men there were not to freeze or starve to death during the winter. Wegener therefore had already decided not to gamble on the motor sledges getting through, and had ordered a fourth dog-sledge journey.)

THE FOURTH SLEDGE JOURNEY
by Dr Fritz Loewe, Aviation Weather Bureau, Berlin

4 September. Wegener ordered Weiken and myself to prepare to take out a big dog sledge party (Wegener planned to send off not less than fifteen sledges) which would definitely ensure the winter supplies reaching Eismitte.

A great difficulty was the getting together of the necessary number of dogs for this big party, say 130. Generally speaking, the best thing to do was to hire the dogs for our summer sledging from the Greenlanders. We had usually to pay about five kroner for the hire of a dog; if a dog died, we usually paid fifteen kroner. The Greenlanders were quite good at palming off on us a number of bad dogs, old dogs, or dogs with vices such as harness-eating, among the good ones. We particularly dreaded the so-called 'pituta-eaters' (pituta is the Eskimo word for dog-traces); their habit of biting through traces and harness made us waste a lot of travelling time in repairs. Leather harness was the most vulnerable, but even yards and yards of hempen cord were devoured, if not digested, by many of the dogs. Often it was only the next day that their crimes were – literally – brought to light, too late for a thrashing to leave any effect on a sledge dog's mind. We tried various means of combating this vice. We dragged the harness through paraffin. In the winter Lissey made leather muzzles, which turned out quite well.

18 September. Wegener had decided that he would lead this journey. He foresaw that important decisions would have to be made and he wished to make them himself. By the evening of 19 September men, dogs, sledges and equipment were all collected at last. The twentieth was spent in the final preparations. On the morning of 21 September our starting-point was a scene of great activity. The dog-teams, already harnessed, were lying about in heaps on the edge of the ice. Often for no obvious reason a dog would throw up its head, open its mouth wide, and howl. First one or two would join in and then the whole chorus, so that an ear-splitting howl resounded over the glacier from a hundred throats. Rising and falling, it would last for several minutes; then there would be a short pause and the chorus would start again louder than ever, until at last even the performers of greatest endurance were silent. We never found out what started off these concerted howlings, which arose from time to time quite independently of external circumstances and are obviously a relic of the old wolf strain in the Eskimo dog. How often we lay in the tent cursing when we could not sleep for it after an exhausting day. Often it was too much even for the ever-cheerful Greenlanders, but they did not know any way of stopping it.

We tried to protect the dogs' feet with 'dogs' kamiks', pieces of sailcloth or sealskin with holes cut for the claws, tied tightly round their legs. The kamiks, however, have to be taken off at every halt of any length, so as to let the dogs lick their paws, and the dogs are also glad to take the chance to eat the kamiks, so that using them is not an unmixed pleasure.

21 September. We had gone barely two miles on the ice-cap and had just reached the crevassed region when we met the third sledge party returning from Eismette: they brought Wegener a letter from the two scientists there, saying they would abandon Eismitte and head back to the coast if no supplies had reached them by 20 October.

23 September. We reached the twenty-five-mile point. The heavily laden sledges made but slow progress on the fresh snow on which we had travelled for the last six miles. On our transport journeys we generally started with a weight of seventy-seven to eighty-eight pounds per dog; with sixty-six pounds reasonable progress might be expected even on a bad surface. Thus a full team could take a load of six to seven cwt. The load gradually diminished, especially as a result of the using up of the dogs' food (each dog got about one pound five ounces daily). On the other hand, we

did not, as has often been done, kill off dogs as the load decreased and use them as food for the rest.

When we were pitching our tents for the night the Greenlanders suddenly raised a shout of 'Kamasuit' ('the big sledge', their name for the motor-sledges). They thought they heard a noise and saw a light to the east. Next morning we saw two tents and one motor sledge a mile or two ahead of us. We went on and met the crews of both sledges and heard all about their experiences. It was no longer possible to count on the motor-sledges reaching Eismitte that year. In view of the slow progress we had been making, we decided to lighten our loads and leave behind everything that was not essential. We depoted no less than sixteen hundredweights here. In the afternoon we saw a veil of uniform grey stratus clouds rising in the west. A snowstorm was threatening. Next morning (25 September) at our camp thirty-one miles out we had thick mist, no wind, and a snowstorm. Silently and steadily the snowflakes fell for two whole days, covering sledges and dogs.

27 September. The weather was sunny and clear with that marvellous clearness which in the outer region of the ice-cap follows the snow. We stuck innumerable times. The wind in our faces increased towards evening and it rapidly grew colder. When we encamped thirty-eight and a half miles out the temperature was −17°F and the east wind was driving the snow before it over the white waste. In the evening all the Greenlanders had collected in one tent. This was a bad sign: something was brewing.

We were right. Next morning (28 September) they all came into our tent. They sat down and said nothing, but stared at the ground and sucked at their pipes. At last their spokesman announced that they all wanted to go home. They had not enough clothes to keep out the cold which was coming and of which they had had a foretaste the day before; the dogs would not be able to pull in the soft snow, and so on. Our attempts to persuade them to change their minds were hindered by language difficulties, and even

Wegener's authority made no impression on the old hunters whom we had with us on this occasion. After a long palaver we finally managed to induce four Greenlanders to go on at a higher rate of pay. The Greenlanders' refusal to proceed further forced us to cut down our effective load very greatly. Once again we had to repack our belongings and thereby lose a day.

On 29 September we parted from the others. Six sledges and sixty-nine dogs with barely two tons of load went on eastwards towards Eismitte, while eight sledges turned back. Day after day we had heavy going through deep snow. By 3 October we had covered seventy-eight miles, by 4 October eighty-seven miles, by 5 October, ninety-four miles. Despite all our exertions we could do barely a mile-and-a-quarter per hour. Our slow progress during the last few days showed us that we had not enough food for ourselves or the dogs to reach Eismitte if the whole party went on. On the other hand, I considered that with the supplies available it was still possible for us to reach Eismitte with one Greenlander, if the other three Greenlanders returned. Finally, on 7 October, Rasmus Villumsen, who had already made two journeys in the interior with me, declared that he was prepared to go on with Wegener and myself. Thus the party divided. The three Greenlanders set off westwards on 7 October. Wegener, Rasmus and I pursued our way eastwards in order to get in touch with Georgi and Sorge if possible, for they had said that they would abandon Eismitte on 20 October if no sledge party had reached them by then.

We made extremely slow progress: by 7 October we had covered ninety-nine miles; by 8 October 103.5 miles; by 9 October 106 miles. The weather was thick, and until 9 October mild. The going was still bad. It was wonderful how Rasmus, who went on ahead, was able to pick out the flags which were almost covered with snow, only a fraction of a square inch showing in a small snowdrift scarcely to be distinguished from any of the others. It was, however, almost impossible to make progress. The dogs on the first sledge were practically swimming belly deep in loose powdery snow. The sledges following got on rather better so long as the runners could be kept in the tracks of the sledge in advance. Often however these could not be followed exactly in the diffuse daylight, or rather twilight, and whenever the sledge slipped sideways off the firm track it immediately sank up to the cross-pieces in the white powder with its load of five cwt. It was then desperate work trying to get it started again; one found oneself wading more than knee-deep in the snow. At last the sledge would move, only to stick fast again in the bottomless snow after a few minutes.

The weather was now colder ($-22°$ to $-40°F$). Wegener felt rather done up after the day before and, contrary to his usual custom, was for waiting, lest we should get our faces frost-bitten in the strong head-wind. On this day of rest – 10 October – we had another long discussion. As regards provisions for ourselves and the dogs the position was more or less as follows. There was food for us for about a fortnight, i.e., with a daily average of nine-and-a-quarter miles it would barely last till we reached Eismitte. With the same rate of progress the dogs' food could be made to last out for the same length of time by gradually cutting down the number of dogs. Both of us were now of the opinion that it was impossible for us to reach Eismitte before Sorge and Georgi started out on 20 October. Wegener went farther and thought that we should not be able to get to Eismitte at all. I too thought that it was unlikely that we should be able to get through in view of the state of our supplies and the time of the year, and I even believed that the danger threatening our party was as great as the danger to Sorge and Georgi. Finally, we decided to make a depot of provisions 143 miles out and turn back.

Next day (11 October) however, the snow conditions improved. In spite of a late start (after days in camp the dogs' harness and traces are invariably in a worse tangle than usual) we managed to cover over six miles with comparative ease. Now it again seemed feasible for us to go on. On 13 October we finally reached the 125-mile point – half way. On 16 October we passed the 143-mile mark. As we were keeping up the daily average on which our plans had been based, we decided to go on. Our retreat now seemed to be cut off.

We often discussed the question whether Sorge and Georgi would leave Eismitte after all. Wegener hoped they would not, while I believed they would, as they had said in their letter, even if they had found meanwhile that it was possible for them to stay on. The journey still went on according to plan. Our effective load was now reduced to one drum of petrol (eight-and-four-fifth gallons), a tent for two, a canvas bucket, a shovel and a lantern. As luck would have it, the only one of these objects, selected after much careful consideration, that was actually used subsequently during the winter was the lantern.

The going was reasonably good as far as about the 174-mile point; after that it actually improved, and beyond the 225-mile point the hard crust due to wind action was often strong enough for the dogs and even a man not to break through. The hollows between the low drifts, however, were filled with soft floury snow, which hindered the sledges very much. Owing to the long duration of the sledge journey, the dogs were beginning to fail in spite of adequate food and light loads. Rasmus always went ahead, although now he had the heaviest load. It is a remarkable fact that although the Greenlanders spared their dogs much less than we did, for example, practically never got off the sledge themselves, they lost fewer dogs.

Our clothes and sleeping-bags were gradually getting wet. The continual work with the dogs' traces had given me slightly frost-bitten fingers – nothing serious, but very painful. My feet were also affected slightly. Wegener, who was more experienced and had a constitution better adapted to Arctic travel, had hitherto escaped getting frost-bitten.

With daily marches of about nine-and-a-quarter miles we reached the 208-mile point on 24 October. We stayed in camp there on 25 October. That day we definitely expected Georgi and Sorge to arrive; and as the temperature now never rose above −40°F, all day long, we had no desire to go on against the fairly strong wind. As dusk fell, as it now did about 4 p.m., and the wind had fallen, we went for a walk together and kept a look-out to the east. But nothing appeared. The livid shadow of the earth crept over the dull white expanse.

While we tramped up and down in front of the tent Wegener spoke openly (as he did but rarely) of his belief that there is purpose behind man's evolution, and that mankind will ultimately be liberated by the growth of knowledge; to contribute to this advance was the ideal which inspired all Wegener's actions. As the darkness meanwhile fell and sledges, dogs and tent lay as dark shadows under the glittering firmament, the gleaming arch of the northern lights, a symbol of such faith as his, led our gaze to its coloured bands and along its mazy forms into infinity.

The rest of the march was a case of 'retreating forwards', chiefly on account of the lack of dogs' food; for we went on from the 208-mile point with only two-and-a-half rations of dogs' food. After this the temperature was about −58°F all the time. The mean temperatures of the days 26 to 30 October were all below −58°F.

On the evening of 27 October I noticed that the toes of both my feet had no feeling in them at all. Wegener immediately began massaging them for hours on end, and continued this morning and evening for the next few days. But it was too late; the circulation could not be started again. During the actual journey, however, they did not inconvenience me at all.

On 28 October, 234 miles inland, we used the last half-ration of dogs' food. On the 29th we were determined to get to Eismitte, but as we lost the flags in the darkness we were forced to camp two or three miles short of it, leaving all our effective load a mile farther back. On the morning of 30 October we had not even any paraffin left; we heated up the last remnant of our provisions, a little black pudding, with 'meta'. We then covered the last few miles in mist at a temperature of −62°F, Rasmus in front, then Wegener, myself last. We reached the station at Eismitte at 11 a.m. on 30 October. We were greeted by Georgi and Sorge, crawled down into the ice-cave, which to us seemed like paradise, and sat for a while quite overcome by its warmth (23°F). Wegener was in excellent form, in high spirits, proud of having carried through this sledge journey successfully, physically, too, he was perfectly fit. Rasmus was also in good condition. I felt rather done-up and a few hours later crawled into my sleeping-bag, in which I was to spend over six months.

(While Wegener and his companions had been making their epic journey to Eismitte, the two scientists there had been adapting to the approach of winter. Here Dr Ernst Sorge, Glaciologist, describes their life as they waited for Wegener to arrive.)

WINTER AT EISMITTE
by Dr Ernst Sorge, Glaciologist

From 13 September, 1930, onwards there were two of us at Eismitte, Georgi as leader and meteorologist, I as his companion and glaciologist. To begin with we lived in the tent, and what with making meteorological observations, sending up pilot balloons, and excavating underground passages and rooms to live in during the winter, we had plenty to keep us busy. Next morning the temperature in the tent was −35°, and we decided we would now retreat underground and seek shelter from the merciless cold − and in this we were successful. In the last few weeks we had excavated underground passages and rooms in the *firn* with a knife, saw and spade.

On 5 October we 'moved in', i.e., we took our equipment into the ice-cave and after that slept there instead of in the tent. The roof of ice, over five feet thick, kept out the cold. In our excavations we left platforms of ice for sleeping-places. The passage leading into the ice-cave was closed by three curtains of sacks, waterproof sheeting and reindeer skins. Our first and strongest impression was that we were lying in state in a crypt. Everything was white like marble, and our sleeping places were clean cut and rectangular like the marble base of a sarcophagus. The last traces of day-light filtered down through the ceiling of ice as a mysterious blue light. In addition we had the dim light of a small lamp which lit up the vault in a ghostly, unreal way, so that it was only extremely gradually that one realised the extent of the space. All this gave a mysterious and rather uncanny impression.

Soon, however, we felt at home in the comfortable room, where no wind penetrated. The small oil-lamp worked very well; Georgi made it out of old tin and glass photographic plates. No one was ever so well acquainted with the *firn* as we were. If we needed ice to make hot water, we cut a piece from the wall. As this process was repeated we at the same time acquired convenient cupboards. If we wanted to throw away slops or other liquids, we merely made a hole in the floor with a ski-stick, poured it in and it vanished without leaving a trace. If our sleeping places were too high or sloped too much, we removed

The observation tower at Eismitte:
when the hut did not arrive the men dug under the snow

our sleeping bag, palliasse and reindeer skins and cut away ice until we were pleased with them.

On 10 October, the temperature fell to −62°. Our breath made a crackling noise like that of a rowing boat moving among reeds or rushes; this was due to the water vapour freezing instantly into small crystals of ice. That evening we went out several times to 'enjoy' the cold − for this was the first time the temperature had gone below −60°F, and besides, there was moonlight and a wonderful starry sky. We were gradually coming to understand Nansen's enthusiasm for the Arctic night.

We waited and waited for the fourth sledge party which was to bring us our winter hut, paraffin and instruments. But no one came. In our letter to Wegener on 13 September we had said that we would start back for the coast on 20 October. We now gave them another week. Still no one came. Now, after thorough consideration, we decided to remain here at Eismitte for the winter, contrary to what we had said. We knew that the Central ice-cap station was one of the principal items in Wegener's programme. So as we now saw that there was a possibility of living through the winter in our ice cave, we stayed where we were. Our chief regret was the absence of the wireless set, without which we had no means of informing our companions of the position we were in. We could only hope that no sledge party was on its way to us, as its members would scarcely escape without frost-bite.

We soon found that our small stove used up more paraffin than we could spare. At first we had it on for ten or twelve hours daily, but by the end of October we had cut this down to an hour or two in the afternoon. On the morning of 30 October we heard a noise up above which without any doubt was made by a dog sledge. Hurrah: they're coming. We jumped out and ran up the steps into the open air. The Greenlander Rasmus Villumsen was there. We led him into the house and pulled off his iced-up furs. In a few minutes Wegener and Loewe arrived too.

We were extremely delighted to see them, but our joy was not an unmixed one, as Loewe's toes, heels and fingers were frozen and blue. He was immediately undressed and put in a dry warm sleeping bag. Georgi and I could not cease to marvel at the almost unbelievable achievement of the party in making a dog-sledge journey against the wind with temperatures about −60°F, and of Loewe in being able to go on marching for the last four days with frost-bitten toes. It seemed almost like a miracle to us that Wegener looked as fresh, happy and fit as if he had just been for a walk. The contrast between the temperature of 23°F in our room and the cold outside was so great and our room was so comfortably arranged, compared to the tent they had travelled with, that Wegener kept exclaiming, 'You are comfortable here, you are comfortable here,' over and over again.

Wegener's energy had not been exhausted by the forty days of hard sledging; on the contrary he was fired with enthusiasm and ready to tackle anything. He was very pleased that we had decided to winter at Eismitte. He would never have ceased to regret it if this station had had to be abandoned. Wegener thought it best that Loewe should remain at Eismitte with us, where he could have rest and attention although we had but few medical supplies, as the return journey might well prove fatal to him. With care the stores at Eismitte could be made to do for three men.

On 1 November we all joined in celebrating Wegener's fiftieth birthday, and then he and Rasmus set off westwards with two sledges and seventeen dogs. It was now warmer (−38°F), half-overcast, with a slight breeze from the south-south-east i.e., splendid sledging weather. The dogs had been pulled down a bit by the cold, but the sledges were light, and with the wind in their favour they set out confidently for the coast. Now we were cut off from the world for half a year, and should have to rely on ourselves and the equipment which lay within twenty yards around us. As the party now consisted of three, a new

*Carrying out a scientific measurement on ice weight and density
in the under-snow work room at Eismitte*

sleeping-place was cut out of the shorter wall of the living room.

In a few days the fate of Loewe's toes was sealed. It was impossible to save them. By 9 November they looked quite shapeless and wasted away; the sinews were sticking up like ridges among the decomposing flesh. Georgi whetted his pocket-knife until it was as thin and sharp as a safety-razor blade. We first tried applying snow at a temperature of 25°F to act as a local anaesthetic, but it appeared to have no effect. Probably the snow was not cold enough, but freezing Loewe's feet again artificially was considered too risky. So finally, Georgi cut away the flesh round the roots of the toes with his sharp knife, nipped off the bones of the second to fifth toes with a metal-cutting shears, and cut through the very sensitive big toe at the softest part. My job was to hold the electric torch and use all my strength to hold Loewe's leg still. Georgi's skill in performing this difficult operation was as amazing as Loewe's brave endurance – for we had no anaesthetics. Afterwards the freely bleeding wounds were washed with chinosol solution and dressed with cotton wool and thin cotton bandages.

As we became better acquainted with the various difficulties that arose and learned how to cope with them, we gradually felt more and more at home in Eismitte. Our life was very much a matter of routine. At 7.20 a.m. by central Greenland time the alarm clock went off. At 7.35 precisely Georgi lit the candle in a small glass lantern, pulled his hood over his head, hung round his neck a brush for cleaning snow off the instruments and an electric torch wrapped in woollen stockings, put on his fur gloves, took the meteorological notebook with pencil attached and hurried out into the dark to make the morning observations of the weather. A quarter of an hour later he would come back, often shouting cheerfully, 'New cold record −68°'.

Meanwhile the ice in the pot had melted, the water came to the boil and Georgi made one of his famous brands of porridge, which were never repeated – and

perhaps never will be. In the course of time we had porridge with prunes, porridge with lemon drops, porridge with chocolate, porridge with coffee, porridge with soup cubes, porridge with left-over bread, porridge with brawn, porridge with dried vegetables, porridge with onions, and porridge with orange peel. Every degree of consistency from very thin to very thick and every kind of mixture was tried. Up to a point the porridge was always a novelty; but there was invariably an unwanted ingredient, namely reindeer hairs, which could not be got rid of so long as we lived in such close contact with reindeer skins and sleeping bags. For this reason it was best to eat one's porridge with a spoon and a pair of tweezers.

Our afternoons were regularly marked off by the meteorological observations at 1.40 p.m. and 8.40 p.m. Writing in ink was out of the question, as the ink immediately froze in great lumps on the pen. From my seat I could reach all the food and cooking utensils, and so I could cook the dinner very comfortably. It usually consisted of tinned meat and vegetables, e.g., goulash, lobscouse, meat roll, corned beef or pemmican. The contents of the tins were naturally frozen as hard as a rock and had to be thawed out over the cooker before the tins could be emptied. A little over two pounds per man per day was not very much at our low temperatures, but we found it sufficient to maintain our strength. On Sundays everyone got an apple or an orange. Our two boxes of fruit stood in the 'store-room', where the temperature was −22°F all the time. Hence the fruit was always frozen hard and when knocked together made a noise like billiard balls. If necessary it was thawed in warm water and tasted quite fresh. We prized the fresh fruit above any of the other things we had to eat.

In the evening we dressed Loewe's wounds; later this was done only every second or third day. We were short of cotton-wool and bandages, so we had to use them sparingly and over and over again. The air was apparently free of germs, so that the wounds got no worse, but in the cold they healed very slowly.

We never caught a cold, however, no matter how cold we felt.

On 24 November Loewe discovered that we had live-stock, namely lice which the Greenlanders of the last dog-sledge party had left behind. In a single night he collected no less than 370 crawling insects. Now we were very much in the same position as men in a dug-out at the front during the War. We lived in much the same way, we were just as dirty and greasy, we had lice, and we were uncertain whether we would get out of it alive. Fortunately the lice found the temperature of our room unbearably cold, so that they were unable to crawl from one sleeping-bag to another. One merely had to throw them on the

Life in the ice cave under the snow at Eismitte: it was so cold even the lice froze

ground and they very soon froze to death. Consequently Georgi and I managed to keep ourselves almost free of them. A very effective way of preventing these charming companions from increasing in numbers too rapidly was to take Loewe's sleeping bag outside fairly often, Loewe meanwhile wrapping himself in rugs. At a temperature of $-58°$ to $-76°F$ all the lice instantly froze to death; they could then be seen very easily and brushed off.

Those who suffered from cold feet got hot water bottles in their sleeping bags. Georgi made one out of a biscuit tin. When filled with hot water and wrapped in a biscuit-bag it rendered us inestimable service.

Once the winter solstice was past we thought the worst was over; from now on the light must steadily improve. From 21 November 1930 to 21 January 1931 we were without the sun. During this time of 'darkness' the sky did get a little lighter about noon, only the brightest of the stars remaining visible. The splendour of the northern lights was indescribable. Thus passed our winter at Eismitte.

It is really impossible to depict our real feelings. Expressed in human language, it was sometimes hope, sometimes despair, defiance or apathy, longing or loneliness. What we shall never forget is that last meeting with Wegener, the continual fight against Nature's supremacy, the uncertainty daily renewed, the passion with which we flung ourselves into our scientific work, and our wonderful comradeship, which in truth always inspired us afresh with firm faith in the success of the Winter station.

(But if the people at Eismitte could settle down to a winter of philosophising and surviving after Wegener had waved farewell, and set off on his return journey, the men awaiting him at Western Station soon had plenty to worry about. During the outward journey to Eismitte, Wegener had written two letters (carried back by members of his disintegrating team) to the man he had left in charge at Western Station, Dr Karl Weiken.)

Thirty-eight-and-a-half-miles inland, 28 Sept. 1930

Dear Weiken,
My fears have been realised. Not only have the motor sledges not got beyond 125 miles, but our sledge party too has broken down owing to the unfavourable weather. Of the twelve Greenlanders eight are returning today. We had great trouble in persuading the other four to stay with us and whether we shall manage to reach the 250-mile station with them remains to be seen. This morning we have a temperature of $-18.8°F$, drifting snow and a head-wind, lovely weather. The whole business is a big catastrophe and there is no use in concealing the fact. It is now a matter of life and death. Best wishes to all, and may we all meet again safe and sound with some satisfactory achievements to look back on.
Alfred Wegener

The second letter was only a little more re-assuring:

Ninety-four miles inland, 6 Oct. 1930

Dear Weiken
The soft deep fresh snow has reduced our rate of marching very much: 1 Oct nine-and-a-quarter miles, 2 Oct nothing, 3 Oct three-and-three-quarter miles, 4 Oct eight-and-three-quarter miles, 5 Oct seven miles. This has made hay of our programme again. We are now sending three Greenlanders home. I had promised each of them a watch from the expedition if they carried on to the 125-mile depot. Seeing that we are now sending them back, please give them the watches they have been promised and see that a watch is put aside for Rasmus, who is going on with us. Please send out a small relief party with dog sledges, say two dog teams and two members of the expedition. The relief party should leave about 10 Nov, and must be prepared to wait at the thirty-eight-and-a-half mile depot until 1 Dec. During the time of waiting perhaps a measurement of the thick-

ness of the ice or some other scientific work could be carried out. We are all well – no frostbites so far – and hopeful of success. Greetings to all.

Alfred Wegener

THE RELIEF JOURNEY
by Dr Karl Weiken

10 November. When we set out with the two Greenlanders, the thermometer was down to −20°F. We had barely covered the nine miles when the storm became so violent that the dogs could make no progress against the drifting snow. So we gave it up and pitched our tents. Next day the storm was nearly as bad. The temperature was −22°. For four days we waited for this storm to die down. It was not until 15 November that we were able to go on. That day at noon we saw the sun for the last time just above the horizon. On the morning of 20 November the drifting had slackened sufficiently to let us risk going on. Soon after that we lost our way again and could not find the thirty-four-mile depot in spite of all our attempts. On 21 November, in spite of heavy drifting, we found the route right away, only to lose it again immediately. We had to reach the thirty-eight-and-a-half-mile depot that day, but there seemed little prospect of our finding it, for we could see barely a hundred yards ahead. Thus at last, after twelve days (on only six of which we had been able to travel), we had succeeded in reaching the point indicated by Alfred Wegener. This was the day, too, on which Wegener should reach it according to his reckoning in his last letter from the ninety-four-mile depot. We found the depot untouched, so Wegener could not have been there already.

From the first day onwards we lit a paraffin flare every afternoon as darkness began to fall, say about 3 p.m.; it lasted for three hours, so that it covered the time during which a party on the move must encamp. We had never had any serious doubt about Wegener

not being able to keep to the times given in his last letter of 6 October.

It was now 1 December, the extreme date given by Wegener. Could Wegener and his companions have perished as a result of exhaustion and unfavourable weather on the way? Wegener's party had now been under way for two and a half months, three times as long as we had, so they might well be more done up. To counter-balance this there were Wegener's energy, his incomparably greater experience, and more careful and efficient habits of travelling. We weighed up all the possibilities, but always came back to the conclusion that Wegener and his companions could not have perished. The longer we waited and considered all the possibilities, the more probable, nay the more certain, did it seem to us that Wegener had stayed to winter at Eismitte. On 6 December the thermometer registered −44°F and a violent storm set in again. We gave up all hope of our companions coming now; we should have to return to the Western station without them.

How different it was with the wind and drifting snow in our backs. We rushed without stopping past cairns and flags which we had not seen at all on the outward journey. We got in at 7 p.m. Without making a special effort, we had covered a distance westward in one day that in the opposite direction had taken us and the dogs twelve days of toilsome struggle. Our companions were glad that we had got back. No one, however, could conceal a certain disappointment that Wegener had not returned. We could do nothing for them before April and could hear nothing of their fate before the end of April. To discourage the feeling of depression, especially in view of the Greenlanders' presence, we played lively records on the gramophone. During the rest of the winter all our strength would have to be devoted to the winter work we had planned. We all felt the absence of Wegener and Loewe, who had meant to spend the winter at the Western station with us. Above all, we were weighed down by our anxiety

93

about the absent ones, and the necessity of sending a sledge party to relieve the Eismitte station and clear up the fate of our companions as early as possible in the spring. It was now 6 December.

THE SPRING SLEDGE JOURNEYS TO EISMITTE
by Dr Karl Weiken

23 April. At last, the first spring sledge journey. It will be devoted to finding out what has become of our companions at Eismitte. Here we have to be prepared for anything, from the possibility of Wegener, Loewe, and Rasmus having perished on the outward journey and Georgi and Sorge on the return journey, to the possibility (which we were all really counting on) of all five of our companions being safe and sound at Eismitte. The start of the dog-sledge party for Eismitte was delayed by a storm which brought much new snow and mist. Wegener's last letter to us the previous autumn had been sent from the ninety-four-mile depot. Of his journey beyond that point we knew nothing. Accordingly, all the way from the ninety-four-mile depot to Eismitte we investigated every detail which might throw any light on Wegener's outward journey and that of any returning party. We found many relics of Wegener's outward journey, but no signs of a party having returned. Everything seemed to indicate that the outward journey had gone according to plan, and that no return journey had been made. Now we scarcely doubted that we should find our five companions safe and sound at Eismitte. Beyond 125 miles the going was quite level and hard, so in spite of our previous exertions we were able to cover the last 109 miles in three days, thereby setting up a record for journeys into the interior which was not again reached.

Next morning we started early in order to reach Eismitte that day. Our thoughts hurry ahead of us to Eismitte. Shall we find all our companions there? And how will they be after the hard winter? I catch sight of the snow castle at Eismitte. We've done it. The castle grows and grows and so does our excitement. Now we shall know all. I see two men only, they wave, my heart is beating like to burst: are there really only two? I leap out and throw my arms round Sorge. In the same breath we both ask, 'Is Wegener with you?' The silent answer tells us both all. I go back to the sledge and realise that the worst has come to pass. In the camp there was a sinister stillness. Then Loewe comes out, bearded and limping, 'Wegener and Rasmus left for the west on the first of November, so they are dead.'

Until early morning we sat together in the ice-cave at Eismitte. Our thoughts and our talk were all of Wegener, our Wegener who was now dead, and his faithful companion Rasmus.

THE FINDING OF ALFRED WEGENER'S BODY
From reports by Dr Karl Weiken

When it was established (on 7 May) that Alfred Wegener and Rasmus Villumsen had perished it was decided to begin the search for the bodies at once.
12 May 1931. Wegener's skis have been found standing upright in the snow with a broken ski-stick midway between them. The point is 132 miles from Eismitte, which Wegener left on 1 November last year – and 118 miles from the Western Station he was heading for. Soon we found reindeer hairs in the snow, then a reindeer skin and Wegener's fur clothing, which was spread on top of a sleeping bag cover. We found Wegener's body sewn up in two sleeping bag covers. It was lying on a sleeping bag and a reindeer skin, two and a half feet below the snow surface of November, 1930. Wegener was fully dressed; he had extra kamiks on his feet and was wearing dog-skin trousers with blue cloth trousers below them, and on the upper part of his body a shirt, a blue ski-ing tunic, a blue waistcoat, his woollen

jacket, a thick sweater, a woollen wind-jacket, woollen helmet, cap and cuffs. The whole of his clothing was in perfect order and free from drifted snow; in particular, the fur boots were soft and firmly stuffed and not iced up.

All these facts indicate that Wegener died not as a result of cold, but probably from heart failure after over-exertion. It is probable that the struggle to keep up with the dog sledge on the up and down surface of November 1930, especially in the dim light, may have led to this overstrain. There were small frost-bites on the nose and hands, such as are usual on journeys like this. Wegener's eyes were open and the expression on his face was calm and peaceful, almost smiling. His face was rather pale, but looked younger than before.

The body was carefully sewn into the bags again by the Greenlanders and laid in the ice just as before.

Above it a vault of large firm blocks of ice was built and covered with a Nansen sledge. When the grave was finished, one of the Greenlanders planted on it a small cross made out of Wegener's broken ski-stick, and we tied a black flag to each of the upstanding skis.

The fate which befell Rasmus, Wegener's Greenlander companion, remains entirely obscure. Either he perished soon after Wegener, in which case his body will every year be buried more and more deeply in snow; or he may have reached the outer part of the ice-cap, in which case his body under favourable conditions may eventually be revealed by the yearly melting of the ice. It is, however, equally possible that he reached the outer part of the ice-cap in a region of large crevasses and that his body lies in some completely inaccessible place, perhaps in a glacier crevasse. He was only twenty-two years of age.

EPILOGUE

Wegener's colleagues continued with their scientific work, and completed their year long survey of the glaciology and meteorology of the great Greenland ice-cap. Their reports filled seven volumes and contained much of that previously unknown knowledge Wegener had so thirsted for; about the jet streams in the upper atmosphere – and the fact the ice-cap was over 3,000 feet thick in places (an utterly unexpected finding).

But as the Arctic summer returned, and the ice started to break up, the expedition members prepared to leave. Wegener himself would stay behind in his ice-tomb, high on the inland plateau, in an area named 'Alfred Wegener Land' in his honour. But his fellow scientists who were also just fellow men, as Wegener himself was, had another world to return to. Here one such scientist – newly a father just before he left Germany to join the expedition – says goodbye in

a way that sums up the feelings of many a traveller at the end of a long, long journey.

'I must close the account of our stay in Greenland by expressing my thanks to all who helped us to carry out our tasks; to the late Professor Alfred Wegener for his inspiration and all that he did to ensure the success of the expedition. Although we have a great longing for home, it is hard to say good-bye .... Greenland's coast vanishes on the horizon, Iceland and the Faeroes come in sight, and finally we are swallowed up in the great city of Copenhagen.

Summer heat glows over the lonely, sandy pine-wood country of Brandenburg, and in front of me stands a little boy, naked but quite unconcerned. When his father went away he was barely three months old, and now in childish language he is telling the strange man what a bath-sponge is for – a very pleasant introduction to the regulated life of civilization in Central Europe.'

Wings over Africa

Sir Alan Cobham was one of the great pioneer aviators. He had learnt to fly with the Royal Flying Corps during the First World War. After the war he was co-founder of the Berkshire Aviation Company, main asset one second-hand Avro Bi-plane, cost £450. With this Cobham went 'barnstorming' round the country – that is giving joy-rides to an aviation-crazy public at one pound her person per flight, from any convenient field he could hire. Aerobatics were also included, and even a little wing-walking – not to mention plenty of unscheduled landings, among them a particularly uncomfortable one in a potato field. . . .

Sir Alan Cobham, the intrepid aviator

But as well as being a man of immense energy, Cobham also had a clear vision of the great future that lay ahead for aviation. It was the means that would draw the distant places of the globe together: transform the weeks taken by the lazy ocean liners into days – even into hours. He could see it clearly: but how to convince a war-weary government – an unimaginative bureaucracy?

Nevertheless, despite all official lack of enthusiasm, he achieved a considerable number of great trail-blazing flights across the world. Outstanding among them is this account of his flight from Croydon to Cape Town and back in 1925; a seventeen-thousand-mile flight in a single-engined aircraft, capable of staying in the air for just six hours at a time before landing to refuel. Its speed was a leisurely 110 mph, its construction fabric, metal and wood – in Africa the tail-skid had to be stood in a tin of paraffin to stop termites eating the air-frame. Yet nothing could stop Cobham: and it is typical of the man that he wrote the book of his flight (from which this account is drawn) in a single week-end – though using three typists.

So without further delay: 'My Flight to the Cape and Back', with Sir Alan Cobham.

TO THE CAPE AND BACK

LONDON TO CAIRO

A journey from London through Egypt and the heart of Africa to Cape Town has for centuries appealed to the world as a great adventure. And so a few years ago, when I contemplated this trip with an aeroplane as my means of transport, everyone looked upon the journey as a somewhat hazardous undertaking. For over four years I had been contemplating the

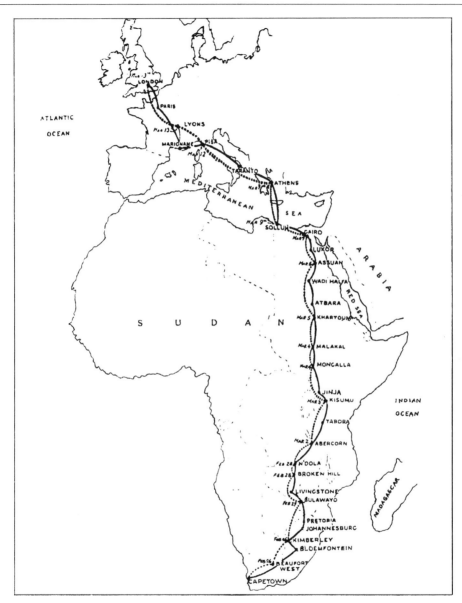

*Map of Sir Alan Cobham's record breaking flight of over
16,000 miles from Croydon to Cape Town and back*

London–Cape Town flight. My progress was always checked when it came to the question of finance, for it was so difficult to persuade any company or individual to finance such a scheme, apart from the fact that it was good long-sighted policy and sound propaganda for British aviation. However, last year I induced twenty-one different companies directly or indirectly connected with aviation to support a flight of survey from London to Cape Town and back.

On my struggles in the summer of 1925 in grappling with the difficulties, not only of getting finance, but of putting down supplies through regions of uncharted territory, organising the preparation of old and disused landing grounds, communicating with hosts of officials and various forwarding agencies, I will not dwell, except to say that in a somewhat impaired condition of health, owing to the terrific worry and work of this organisation, by 15 November I found myself ready to start.

In the light of my experiences on a recent previous flight from London to Rangoon and back, I came to the conclusion that I could select no better craft for this occasion than that which I used on the Rangoon expedition, namely a De Havilland type 50. For those who have never seen the De Havilland type 50, let me give a brief outline of the machine. It is a biplane – that is, it has four wings and a body – and the passenger cabin is immediately behind the engine, and between the upper and lower planes. The pilot's cockpit is separate and right behind the cabin, but there is a little communicating window inside the cockpit to the rear of the cabin, so that it was possible for me to converse with my crew during flight. The pilot's seat is high up, so that when the machine was in flight I had an uninterrupted view ahead, over the top of the cabin in front of me.

For the Cape flight I decided to have installed a 385 H.P. Siddeley Jaguar, which is an air-cooled

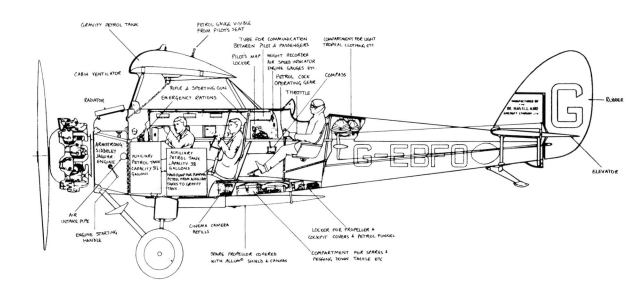

Sectional diagram showing internal arrangements of the D.H. 50

engine. This gave me a speed of about 110 mph and a petrol capacity of some six hours. Before telling the tale of our adventures I must introduce the other two members of the expedition, Mr A. B. Elliott, who was the engineer on the Rangoon flight, and who had been with me on many other occasions, was the engineer on this trip also. It had been decided that a cinematograph film should be made of the whole venture so that the British public might share in a minor degree all our experiences. Thus it came about that the Gaumont Company selected Mr B. W. G. Emmott from their staff to come with us to make the picture.

Our departure from Stag Lane Aerodrome was of great interest and no little amusement to those who saw us off. Stowing the spares, luggage and equipment on board seemed to be the chief business of the day. Firstly we carried underneath the cabin a spare propeller. Then Emmott seemed to have a terrific amount of camera gear to pack away. Then again we had guns to go on board, because I came to the conclusion that, should we by any misfortune have to land in some uninhabited country or tractless jungle, the guns would not only be a protection but might be our only means of getting food. Therefore we carried a gun, a rifle and a revolver. There were the emergency cooking utensils, consisting of very light aluminium kettle, pots, mugs and frying pan, besides light aluminium water bottles, and emergency rations in the form of compressed food.

Considerable excitement prevailed when, on that cold grey November morning, three large pith sun helmets were stowed in a special compartment in the back of the machine, with a parcel containing mosquito nets. I think too, that Emmott's and Elliott's light flannel suits and my own khaki drill caused a good deal of comment, but we had heavy underwear and heavy overcoats to keep us warm until we were out of Europe.

Our baggage had been cut down to the finest limits; we each had one suitcase which when full weighed not more than twenty pounds and measured about twenty inches long by fourteen inches wide and six inches deep. However, there was room for a light alpaca dinner-jacket and evening accessories, so that we could appear more or less respectable when occasion demanded.

After that we were all ready for the start; in fact I was getting somewhat impatient to get away, for I am never very keen on the 'official good-bye' business. Perhaps my impatience accounted for the fact that I opened my engine a little too quickly as I was taking off on that very cold morning, and consequently momentarily choked her, so that I had to shut off and open out again more slowly. With our reserve of power, however, we were in the air like a rocket, only too thankful to be away at last. On the first day we only reached Paris, and refrained from carrying on to Lyons, because I felt that we were all so tired after the final rush of getting away – though there were others who said we could not resist the temptation of a night in Paris. On the following day we flew on to Lyons in indifferent weather, and as the hour was too late for us to make Pisa, our intended next stop, we pushed on to Marseilles instead and there spent the night. Bad weather welcomed us next morning, but after it had cleared a little we flew on again for Pisa.

The sky was overcast and grey, while the Alps were buried in low cloud and mist: but the weather condition which caused us real trouble was the violent, strong north-east wind which for hundreds of miles was dashing over these ice-clad peaks. The result was that by the time the gale had reached the Mediterranean the whole atmosphere seemed to be carried in one mighty chopped-up downrush to the sea.

The further we proceeded along the coastline the more violent became the atmosphere, and so I thought that by flying low under the cliff we might possibly avoid the main disturbance; but here the down current was so violent that it was difficult to keep the machine on an even keel. I then decided to climb to a high altitude in search of a calmer zone so, opening out the engine and pulling back the control lever, we very quickly shot up to 6,000 feet. But the higher we went the worse became the bumps, and the machine at times seemed to be almost uncontrollable. Emmott and Elliott in the cabin were having a very rough time, for it was with great difficulty that they could keep in their seats. While Elliott strove to keep the baggage in position, Emmott was struggling with his beloved camera which I thought might be broken at any moment, as very often baggage and passengers' heads touched the roof of the cabin as the machine was caught in some violent down current.

All this took place in a very short space of time and we quickly decided that the only course of action was to get away from the trouble, the mountains; and so we headed for the open sea. This was not sufficient to get rid of all the bumps, and I resorted to an old plan that I had practised often before; we flew right out to sea, away from the shore and very low over the water, which evidently acts as a cushion for the down currents of the wind, and gives a more or less steady, even atmosphere. In this way we continued across the bay before Genoa, skimming over the sea within twenty feet of the water, in fact so low were we flying

Members of the expedition: A. J. Cobham, R. W. G. Emmott and A. B. Elliott

that when we encountered a fleet of fishing smacks it was necessary to climb a little to clear their masts. It was here we had the little thrill of flashing by these boats as they were tossed in the rough sea, much to the excitement of the fishermen who waved vigorously to us as we flew on our way.

On the following day we had a comparatively simple flight over almost the whole length of Italy to Taranto at the heel of Italy. Here we were most enthusiastically received by the Italian Commandant who greeted us the moment we landed, while in his trail followed one of the mess stewards, carrying a tray of bottles and glasses with all the requirements necessary for any cocktail that one might mention. We had travelled 500 miles or over 800 kilometres, and our host evidently considered that we needed fortifying. He himself mixed for us some wonderful brandy flip cocktails, whose main ingredients were eggs and brandy, and after partaking of them we all had a distinctly good impression.

On the following day we set out on our trip from the heel of Italy to Athens. Again we had to resort to our old tactics of flying low over the sea. From Athens we had a 480-mile flight over the sea by way of Crete to Sollum on the African coast, and thence eastwards along the sea shore to Cairo. At Athens Elliott decided to give the engine a thorough inspection for the sake of safety during our long crossing to Sollum, and we were appalled to find that all the pistons were beginning to disintegrate. This created an embarrassing problem. Sir John Siddeley had lent us our Jaguar engine for the sake of publicity; he wanted motorists to be impressed with the reliability of his firm's products. I knew perfectly well that it had been fitted with low-compression pistons so as to cope with the low-grade petrol that was going to be available on this flight; what I didn't know was that these pistons were an old set, not made specially, and I was amazed when Elliott now told me this. Here we were, stuck with engine failure almost at the beginning of our journey.

Sir John responded instantly to my carefully-worded cable, though it reached him on Saturday evening. Cars were sent round Coventry, his people were dragged away from their weekend rest and set to work overtime, and by the Tuesday evening a new set of fourteen pistons was ready. They reached us by rail and steamer on the Thursday morning, we installed them and tested the aircraft on the Friday, and on the Saturday we enjoyed a pleasant and completely trouble-free flight to Sollum.

Before leaving England we had a short experimental flight round Stag Lane Aerodrome, when Emmott had evidently imagined that all the facilities for taking pictures were quite simple and in order. Before taking off from Sollum we arranged that one of our first shots would be of the desert changing suddenly from the barren sandy waste to the rich fertile delta of the Nile, to be followed by a long shot of the Pyramids in the distance, after which we would take close-ups of them.

As we neared Cairo on a certain afternoon in December the day began to warm up and, because we had not cast our winter clothing and had just come from a very cold climate, we all felt the sudden heat, especially those in the cabin. On approaching the Nile delta I yelled through my little window into the cabin to tell them to get ready to take pictures, and then the fun commenced. Whether it was that Emmott did not quite understand that it was necessary to wait until the pilot gave him the picture – for the slightest movement of the control lever would take his object out of view – or that neither he nor Elliott were used to working together in such a confined space, or that it was the heat of the day which overpowered them, or yet again that I was at fault for manoeuvring the machine too fast, none of us seemed to know exactly. However, from the onset I could see that something was amiss in the cabin; no one seemed to take pictures when I gave the view, but film was being taken when I was not placing the aeroplane for any particular picture. I throttled down

The first aerial pictures ever taken of the pyramids

the engine and yelled further instructions through the cabin window amid the roar. The only effect that this procedure seemed to have was to darken the countenances of my two passengers, resulting in a further obstinacy to coincide with my manoeuvres for aerial photography.

On nearing the Pyramids I thought that our chance had come for really fine stuff, and after banking the machine and struggling to the best of my ability for two or three minutes to get what I thought would be a magnificent view of this ancient Egyptian masterpiece, I yelled to Emmott to 'take'. On looking through the cabin window I discovered that he had evidently given up the idea of photography, and was gazing vacantly at the landscape, while Elliott, on the other hand, instead of waiting until I had placed the machine in a convenient position for him, was evidently exposing film on a more or less blank desert. This was my turn to become annoyed, for the day was hot and I was beginning to perspire in my winter attire through the exertions of banking the machine round and round the Pyramids. So I shouted through in my lustiest tones to Elliott to 'wait for it' and to Emmott to 'take, take, take'.

Instead of stimulating Emmott to action and modifying Elliott to patience, the effect of my shouting had the most alarming results in the cabin. Two perspiring faces turned round and scowled darkly at me, then scowled at one another; then above the roar of the engine I again shouted to explain matters, whereupon they shouted, and for a few moments a perfect inferno raged. It dawned upon me that possibly I might be to blame for not having arranged with my assistants beforehand and impressed upon them some sound system of co-operation for the aerial photography work, apart from the scanty chat that we had on this subject before starting. Giving up the question of aerial photography for that day, I headed across Cairo for Heliopolis and landed on the R.A.F. aerodrome.

When the machine came to a standstill, I quickly divested myself of some of my outward clothing and was about to explain matters to my crew, when I discovered that both of them, looking very hot, limp and exhausted, had no particular desire to talk to me. However, that was shortlived, because the machine had to be put away and the general routine of the day's work gone through and in the quiet of the hotel that evening we rehearsed with cool and collected heads exactly how our photographic work should be done in the future.

Two days later we started off on a short flight over Cairo to film the Pyramids properly, and on this occasion our system worked perfectly. Having decided who should take the first picture, I yelled through to the cabin, 'Emmott, prepare to take', whereupon he would turn the handle as soon as the object came into view, and I would do my utmost to keep the object within his camera sights, at the same time placing the machine so that sun would throw up the best shadows. Then Elliott would be warned and the machine would be placed for his particular view; in this way the procedure was carried out systematically until the subject had been covered by both cine' and still camera.

We discovered a novel method of filming the Pyramids, keeping them in the picture by a system of side-slipping on to them. Owing to the fact that Emmott was taking his film from the front windows of the cabin, we shall be able to give the public a fine view of the Pyramids looking like tiny piles of masonry from thousands of feet above, then through side-slipping down onto them they gradually get larger and larger until at last they fill the picture – the moment when we had to turn away or side-slip into them.

CAIRO TO CAPE TOWN

After nearly a week in Cairo we took off and flew on down the Nile, over the land of the Ancients, for Luxor; for Emmott was keen not only to get aerial views of Thebes, Karnak, the Temples of Luxor, the Valley of the Kings, and the Ramasseum, but also to get ground pictures of the relics of the Ancient Egyptian civilization.

In these few pages it would be impossible to tell our experiences on every portion of the flight, so I will hurry on to some of my most striking impressions of the journey. We spent our Christmas at Khartoum, and before the old year had departed we flew on our way southwards to the next landing ground at Malakal.

Daily I became more impressed with the enormous opportunities of a great commercial airway that would link up Central Africa with the Mediterranean. Here was a country where it would be possible to maintain a 100% efficiency regularity, and at the same time do a trip in two days that by the present modes of transport takes over three weeks.

At Malakal we landed beside the river on a strip of ground that had been specially prepared but a few weeks before. On the borders of the landing ground was a village of the Shulluks. In order to give our machine as much protection as possible from any gales that might occur, we draw it close up to their huts; curiously, they showed no interest whatsoever in our aeroplane, and I was told they looked upon it as 'one of the mad things the white men do'.

One of the officials told me that an improvement at which these natives really marvel is the installation of water in pipes. For centuries their womenfolk have journeyed night and morning from the village to the river bank to fetch water, and when water pipes were first laid it was a common thing to see natives gathered round the tap, while one, a little more courageous than the rest, would turn the tap and let the water gush out; this to them was truly marvellous. Water was something that they understood and was the main part of their daily existence, so when it could be obtained merely by the turning of a tap, that indeed it was something wonderful. As for an aeroplane, as far as they were concerned it was simply some madness that was not worth considering.

Our next trip was to Mongalla, and the route lay right over the great Sud area which is a vast swamp in the Southern Sudan through which the Nile somehow finds its way. Little was known of the route that we

should take, and I had heard many tales of the desolate nature of the country over which we should have to pass; but, by keeping well eastward of the Nile, I found that the main portions of the great swamps could be avoided. When we were within a few miles of Mongalla, Elliott spotted a herd of water buck on the far side of the Nile and, thinking it would make a good picture for Emmott, I flew over in their direction and came down low in an endeavour to get a close-up picture. The country at this point was open and free from trees and we were able to fly within twenty feet of the ground, Emmott turning the handle of his machine all the while in the hope of getting a really fine picture of the herd.

At Mongalla the heat was terrific and at times the wind seemed like tongues of flame fanning one's face, until one longed for sundown when it started to cool a little. The extraordinary thing was that the aeroplane stood up to this gruelling treatment, despite the

Shulluks at Malakal

fact that it was impossible to touch it without burning one's fingers, and when we took off at last from Mongalla, its performance seemed in no way to have depreciated owing to its exposure to the sun.

Mongalla was the last of our low altitude aerodromes, for it was 1,000 feet above sea level, whereas our next stopping place, Jinja, was over 4,000 feet above sea level. This quick change in the altitude of the landing grounds was almost instrumental in causing an accident. Just as I was coming in low over a banana grove, which bordered the landing ground, several natives rushed across my fairway at the last moment. Thinking that I should most certainly run into them, I did what I should have done at home or in Europe and landed a little bit shorter, with the object of pulling up before I reached them. Landing shorter meant landing slower, and in the sudden moment of emergency I forgot that I was well over 4,000 feet above sea level in a rarefied atmosphere with a conse-

quently much higher flying speed necessary to keep me in the air. The result was that when I pulled out of my little side-slip my machine literally fell out of the air for the last ten feet, and it was only the robustness of the undercarriage that saved the situation.

From Jinja we flew on round the lake to Kisumu which is about five miles south of the equator. We were always being surprised by the startling lack of knowledge of even the simplest rudiments of flying displayed by the various people that we met en route, and many are the stories that we could tell in connection with this topic. The remark of one dear lady at Kisumu is well worth mentioning. After asking me a few perfectly obvious questions about flying, she then said, 'How do you manage to sleep at night?' I replied, 'Oh, we always manage to get put up by the local authorities, either staying in a rest house or enjoying the hospitality of somebody's private residence.' The good lady looked bewildered for a

SPEAR CHARGE
AT AEROPLANE.

—◆—

WARRIORS DANCE ROUND
MR. COBHAM.

—◆—

FROM MR. ALAN J. COBHAM.
the distinguished British airman who has flown 4,545 miles on his 8,000-miles flight from London to Capetown.

moment, and then, with a somewhat disappointed expression on her face, remarked, 'Oh, so you come down at night then.'

Kisumu was virtually the end of our survey of the great air line of the future that will run from Cairo to the Victoria Nyanza, thus bringing the whole of Central Africa within about seven days of England, instead of a month as at present. After my flight over this route I felt that it would be a sound and practical proposition, not only from an aviation point of view but also commercially, to open up one of the finest air transport routes of the age.

From Kisumu we entered the dense forest areas that stretch for hundreds of miles in all directions. We were getting into the rainy season now and, having no personal experience of the climatic conditions of the country, I went forward with considerable caution. I think that this section of the route, from about the south end of the Victoria Nyanza, was the worst stretch of our whole flight from London to Cape Town; it was more or less over dense forest the entire way and, except for the prepared landing grounds, for at least ninety-eight per cent of the journey there was nothing but tree-tops on which it would be possible to land a machine.

My landing grounds in this part of the world, for reasons of economy, were clearings that consisted of two runways 600 yards long and fifty yards wide in the form of a cross, thus making it possible for me to land into four directions of the wind whatever it might be. My original instructions had been that a smoke fire should be lighted immediately the aeroplane was sighted in order that the drift of the smoke would show me the direction of the wind so that I might land head into it.

It is quite simple to imagine what a terrific landmark a landing ground of this nature must have been in the middle of a thick forest, especially when four great smoke fires were lit at each end of the cross. I believe I could see it twenty miles off, all the more easily because there were special white markings on the runways. One official, however, had had many doubts as to whether I should spot the landing ground or not, for soon after we had come down and I had stepped out of the machine, he said to me, 'Could you see the landing ground all right?' Whereupon I replied, 'Perfectly,' and he again remarked, 'By gad, when you flew by here in a circle I thought you had missed it, and I tried to attract your attention. Did you see me wave my hat?'

From N'Dola we went southward. Here we had one of our greatest adventures of the whole trip. We had left Broken Hill early in the morning, and after a 300-mile flight southward along the railway line, I could see dimly on the horizon, above the forest, what appeared to be the smoke from two or three fires. Then gradually it dawned upon me that this was not smoke at all, but clouds of spray rising from the great Victoria Falls.

Presently the River Zambesi could be seen flowing eastwards through the forest until it took a half-right turn, and suddenly disappeared from view; this was where it toppled over the brink of the chasm. We did not trouble to land straight away at Livingstone, although we could see the crowds waiting at our temporary landing ground, but carried on a few miles further to the Falls, aware that this was going to be one of the greatest spectacles of our whole flight. The Zambesi at this point is well over a mile wide and as we approached from the north, all that we could see was a long clean-cut line where the river disappeared into the earth, whence huge clouds of spray were continually rising. In a few moments we had flown beyond the brink. I looked behind and had my first glimpse of the vast volume of water, a mile and a quarter wide, falling from a height nearly as great as that of the cross of St Paul's Cathedral into a deep chasm from which there is only one small gorge outlet. The native name of the Falls when translated is 'Smoke Falls', a title inspired by the banks of smoke-like spray which rise night and day from the ravine. The constantly rising current of air forces the

The Victoria Falls from the air

fine spray up in cloudbanks to a height of over 1,000 feet above the brink of the Falls.

We were lucky to arrive just before the flood season, for the spray is then so heavy that it is often impossible to get a view of the cascade. As it was, both Emmott and Elliott were able to take excellent pictures in between the constantly rising banks. Emmott finally wanted to take a real close-up picture of the brink, so I went to the western end and prepared to fly eastward along the edge of the Falls, so that with the sun nicely behind us Emmott might get a perfect forward view from the port window of the cabin. Since the Falls are a mile and a quarter wide, by flying very slowly and taking a long approach, we reckoned that there would be at least two minutes filming to be done.

From about 500 feet we took a picture of the long line of Falls ahead of us; coming lower we got a close-up of the famous Devil's Cataract at the extreme western end, and then continued flying along the Falls about fifty feet above and fifty yards away from the brink. We had been going but a few seconds when suddenly a cloud of spray enveloped us, and although this was only momentary, we emerged with our wings dripping with water. I looked through the cabin window and noticed that Emmott was turning the handle of his camera with a precision and intentness that I had rarely seen before, for this was the real stuff. A few seconds later, and we were enveloped in another bank of spray, receiving a slight bump as we passed through it. The far end of the brink was almost reached when we flew through a third cloud of fine spray that was denser than all the rest.

At this moment we were directly above the chasm, while ahead were rocky crags: so that when at this moment our engine spluttered – cut out for the first time since we had left London – it was naturally a startling experience. She quickly picked up again, but only for a few seconds before further spluttering. Our engine continued to splutter, miss and bang, and both Elliott and I knew what had happened. As I looked through the cabin window and saw his somewhat troubled countenance, I shaped the word 'water' with my lips. In flying so close to the brink of the Falls the spray, heavier than we had anticipated, had evidently been sucked through our air-intake pipes into our carburettor. It was imperative to keep the engine running and the propeller turning over so that there might be sufficient momentum to carry the engine on when the globules of water were passing through the jet; that is why we opened full out and climbed as high as possible, until at last we were within gliding distance of our landing ground and knew that we were safe should the water prove too much for the carburation. By the time we had reached our landing ground the water apparently had been cleared from the carburettor, for we were running quite regularly again. The only person who was not perturbed by the occurrence was Emmott, who seemed oblivious to the fact that anything was wrong, and had been far too busy to worry about engine troubles in the excitement of turning the handle on so thrilling a spectacle. Despite this reassuring attitude, I made a mental note that never again would I fly low over the Victoria

Falls and dash through its spray banks in an aeroplane; one felt that with a little more water a submarine would be more suitable for the job.

That evening our host suggested that as it was a full moon we should journey once more to the Falls to see the lunar rainbow, a rare sight that occurs only at certain seasons of the year. We motored down on our third visit to the Falls that day, and leaving the car on the roadway, wended our way through a grove of trees to the brink of the cliff at the eastern end of the ravine. There before us was the great silvery grey mass, falling into the dark depths of the gorge, and then as the moon came out from behind a small cloud we had a vision more wonderful than we had seen during the whole day. There appeared what seemed to be the ghost of the rainbow that we had seen in the sunshine. The gentle tinting and colouring of this lunar rainbow had its own mystic charm, and as we all stood gazing in silence upon this beautiful sight I mused over the events of the day and fully realised the foundation and origin of all the native legends and mystery stories that have been handed down from generation to generation about the great Victoria Falls.

The next stop after Livingstone was Bulawayo, where we received our first really big reception and I began to realise how important was our task for the good of British aviation and how imperative it was that we should carry the work through successfully.

After lunching with the local inhabitants and those who had come scores of miles from the surrounding districts to see our machine, we flew on. It struck me very forcibly, after flying for 100 miles how the perpetual forest country suddenly ended and we found ourselves flying over beautiful open rolling plains, with here and there a mountain range; and I soon learnt that this type of country, so perfect for aviation, extended right the way to the Cape.

At Johannesburg we received the greatest reception of all, for over 5,000 people had assembled to witness our arrival, and there were more than 1,000 cars parked on the edge of the landing ground. It was in Johannesburg that our aviation propaganda work started in real earnest; it was found necessary for me to employ two secretaries to keep pace with the correspondence, and very often I had to put in eighteen hours a day in order to fulfil my appointments and complete the work there was to do. Four and five speeches a day were not uncommon, for every society and club wished to hear a few words about aviation and our particular experiences.

The last hop of the long journey was to Cape Town. And that is perhaps best described in the newspaper headlines of the day. They said:

'MR COBHAM REACHES CAPETOWN'
8,020 MILES IN 3¾ DAYS FLYING TIME
HIS GREATEST EXPLOIT
BRITISH AEROPLANE AND ENGINE
PARLIAMENT RISES EARLY TO SEE ARRIVAL.

'Mr Alan J. Cobham successfully completed his great flight this evening, thereby establishing a record as the first man to fly from London to Capetown in the same machine. He arrived over the city at 6.10 p.m. and thrilled spectators for twenty minutes while he circled over the bay, the city, Table Mountain. The airman then wheeled towards the southern suburbs and descended to the aerodrome where he was greeted by the thunderous cheers of an enormous crowd.'

For my own part I wrote:
'We have thus completed a journey of more than 8,000 miles from London over Europe, Egypt and tropical Africa to Capetown with the same Siddeley–Jaguar engine and De Havilland aeroplane, surveying for Imperial Airways this Empire air route. The whole journey was accomplished in ninety-one flying hours. It is interesting to note that the apparatus used was British throughout.' So ended the first half of my flight to the Cape – and back.

CAPE TOWN TO LONDON

Our job of survey over and with a complete knowledge of the route and the allocation of our supplies, we determined to do our utmost to make a speedy flight home, Elliott having overhauled the engine during our stay at Cape Town. It so happened that, on the very day we left, the steamship Windsor Castle was sailing for Southampton, and a sort of impromptu race was started in which the competitors were the Windsor Castle with Captain Strong 'up' versus the De Havilland aeroplane with Alan Cobham 'up'. The Windsor Castle route was one of 5,300 miles, steaming day and night, against ours of 8,500, in which we had to come down at twenty-six different landing grounds, and as a rule could not do more than eight hours flying a day. So the race was going to be a keen one, and I heard afterwards that much money changed hands in consequence.

At 6.45 a.m. on 26 February we were in the air. On this flight we ran into our first real tropical rain storms. We passed through continual downpours on our compass course and I have vivid recollections of flying in mist and rain over trackless forest and miles of uncharted territory. There were whole ranges of mountains, ravines and rivers of which there was no mark whatsoever on our map – the best that could be procured. We went to bed early that night with the intention of getting off at dawn the following morning, but the Fates decided otherwise. In the early hours of the following morning a storm started and five inches of rain fell in the space of four hours. This was too much for our landing ground, and it made the earth so soft that our wheels sank too deep in the mud for us to get up sufficient speed for taking off. We tried time and again, but it was a risky business and we feared that our wheels might suddenly sink too deeply and tip the machine up.

The following morning we again tried our luck, but before doing so we enlisted the services of about a thousand natives from the surrounding villages;

headed by their leader, these marched en masse up and down our fairway chanting and stamping all the while, with the object of making the ground more solid. We got off safely and we were all very thankful.

Elliott we left entirely free on the whole of our flight homewards from Cape Town to London to do nothing but inspect and attend to the maintenance of his engine. This was partly due to the fact that he had contracted malaria fever on the outward journey and had been a whole week in bed during our stay at Johannesburg. Therefore we considered that he was still in a state of convalescence and should not be taxed with any undue form of physical exertion.

Four days later we reached Khartoum, having sometimes flown over 700 miles in a single day. That night a bad sandstorm blew from the north. With the worst of the storm over, we took off from Khartoum on the following morning and started to climb through dust-laden air; at 5,000 feet we were still in the sandstorm, and so climbed on until at 11,000 feet we were not completely out of the dust for there were still banks of fine sand floating above us at that altitude. As we flew our visibility was nil, except when we looked immediately beneath us and could dimly see, passing across the yellow sand some 10,000 feet below, a broad dark shadow that was the Nile.

This was our only guide, for it was unsafe to go on a compass course, because if the weather became too bad and forced us to land in the desert, we should be lost and never found. Suddenly I discovered that the dim shadow I was following on the ground was not the River Nile, and at 12,000 feet in an awful moment I realised that we were for the time lost. Ahead and around us were yellow banks of dust clouds, and beneath we could dimly discern the earth which was the desert. A few moments previously I felt positive that I had seen the river below to the west, so I dived earthwards to find it. Minutes passed and many miles were covered as we dived down and down in search of our only hope. When at last we

were within but a few hundred feet of the ground and still no Nile was in sight, the terrible calamity of the situation dawned upon me; it was impossible to know which way to fly to reach habitation or life of any sort, it was useless to fly on and hopeless for us to land. At this moment luckily I spotted an old dried-up waterway such as one sees in the desert. Ascertaining which way the ancient flow had been, I followed the dry river bed downwards for a few minutes, which seemed like hours, when suddenly the Nile came into view.

After this experience, dust or no dust, we flew twenty feet above the railway line to make sure of keeping it in sight, the river and railway here running side by side. As we neared Abu Hamed the dust became thicker, but our engine ran perfectly in spite of it. Skimming along within a few feet of the earth at 110 miles per hour became extremely fatiguing, and instinctively we throttled back and went slower so that the telegraph poles did not fly by so quickly in a bewildering blur.

On Sunday we took off on the last lap of our flight to Cairo and passed over the old and familiar sites of Thebes, Luxor, Karnak and Assuit. On landing at Heliopolis we were given a hearty reception by the R.A.F.

We had been successful in accomplishing the flight from the Cape to Cairo for the first time in history, and we had taken nine days to do it. Four days later we reached Athens, having been delayed by gales. From Athens we intended to make a final dash home. We flew 360 miles to Taranto at the heel of Italy, filled up, enjoyed an alfresco lunch and made another 500 miles to Pisa.

The next morning we were up early again with the intention of flying via the Riviera coastline to Lyons, but on account of perfect weather conditions I decided to cross the Alps by way of Turin and the Modane Pass. Our passage over the Alps was probably one of the most beautiful flights of the whole trip and, whereas it would have been possible to clear the

MR. COBHAM DUE HOME TO-DAY.

BETWEEN 4 AND 5 P.M.

WHERE TO SEE HIM.

GREAT WELCOME PLANS.

FLIGHT OF 840 MILES YESTERDAY.

Mr. Alan Cobham, the distinguished British airman, is expected at Croydon Aerodrome between 4 and 5 o'clock this afternoon on the completion of his 16,000 miles' flight to Capetown and back.

THE KING
AND
MR. COBHAM

A LONG TALK ON
AIR EXPLOIT

HIS MAJESTY SENDS
FOR MRS. COBHAM.

FINAL DASH OVER ALPS

Arriving over Croydon: Sir Alan Cobham

Pass at 8,000 feet, we cruised over in the wonderful clear morning air at 12,000 feet, surrounded on all sides by the hundreds of glistening snow-covered peaks of the Alps.

We landed at Lyons and after refuelling, dispatching wires, and partaking of coffee and rolls, we set off on the last lap of our 17,000 mile journey. The flight from Lyons to London is about 480 miles; I had to push the engine a little because we encountered a somewhat contrary wind, and I wished to arrive at Croydon at 4 p.m. as I had telegraphed. We flew low over Paris, crossed the Channel, and then at Sevenoaks were met by a whole host of aeroplanes in the air. There were six Moth machines and in one Mrs Cobham, piloted by Capt. de Havilland, had come out to meet us. Very soon a formation was formed about us and thus we arrived at Croydon.

We were all surprised and somewhat overwhelmed at the reception we received, and it seemed that we should never be able to get away from the aerodrome again. I had a letter on board the machine from the Earl of Athlone, Governor and Commander-in-Chief of the Union of South Africa, addressed to His Majesty the King. I enquired how and when I should

113

deliver this letter, and soon received instructions to go to Buckingham Palace as quickly as possible. So off we flew to Stag Lane, and from there we went by car to Buckingham Palace. I was taken to the King's private study: and I shall never forget the moment when George V came forward with outstretched hand and said, 'Congratulations, Cobham, magnificent show: now sit down and tell me all about it'. I soon discovered how keen was His Majesty on the subject of aviation; he asked me many questions regarding our experiences, and I was surprised to find what an insight he had into our flight.

In conclusion let me say that we all felt that the flight from London to Cape Town and back had been worthwhile. Emmott was satisfied that he had a picture which would give the public a vivid idea of our experiences. Elliott was happy because the Siddeley–Jaguar engine had proved a huge success and the De Havilland aeroplane was as good as when it started. Personally I was content that my report on aviation possibilities between London and Cape Town and my report on the behaviour of the machine and engine would be of great use to British aviation at large.

But the telegram which pleased me most read, 'Hearty congratulations on your splendid success from owners and all on board the Windsor Castle. Captain Strong'. I had beaten him by two days and won the race, and this was going to earn me a good lunch before long. Good lunches aren't so rare. What pleased me was the symbolism of this victory. Long-distance travel was then dominated by the ocean liner, which was unbeatable as regards elegance, space and comfort. But I had now offered dramatic proof that it faced a serious challenge in the matter of speed, and speed is what most travellers want. Civil air transport was the coming thing. I had made my point.

Storm, Cape Horn

Irving Johnson, later Captain Irving Johnson, was brought up on a farm in Connecticut, and having heard that many skippers, if they could not get a seaman, would choose a farm boy as the next best thing, determined to go to sea on leaving Princeton University. His preparations for his new life consisted in learning to fight, so that he wouldn't have to, and climbing every telegraph pole within half a mile of his home and then standing on his head on top of it – to overcome his fear of heights.

In 1929 he came to England, and then crossed to Ireland where he visited the Giant's Causeway with his friend Charlie. His hat blew into the sea; at a nearby wishing well, he made a wish for its return, and it came in with the tide. Seeing that 'the wishing apparatus worked', he made a further wish, 'for plenty of exciting storms on our voyage round Cape Horn'. Johnson, with his friend Charlie, then crossed to Hamburg where they were to join the four masted barque *Peking* with its German Captain and crew to make the eleven thousand-mile journey through the English Channel, south with the Trade wind, through the belt of the Doldrums, past the Falklands and round Cape Horn.

'The *Peking* was queen of the seas, and she knew it' and, with her sister ships the *Parmir* and *Passat* represented the final stage in the evolution of the square rigged merchant vessel. She had been built of steel by Blohm and Voss of Hamburg in 1911 for the firm of F. Laeisz, and was designed to carry general cargoes round Cape Horn to Chile and return laden with nitrates. As Johnson said, 'Cargo is king, the ship's only reason for being is one thing – to carry cargo and deliver it in good condition and on time'.

The *Peking* could carry 5,300 tons of cargo in a ship displacing 3,000 tons. She was 345 feet long overall and her mainmast 170 feet, 'the height of a seventeen storey building'. She could set an acre of canvas and her three lower sails weighed a ton each when dry. During the 1914 war she had been stranded in Valparaiso, and after Germany's defeat had been allocated to Italy. In 1921 she was brought back to Europe, re-purchased by her original owners, F. Laeisz, for £8,500, and returned to the nitrate trade.

It was at this period of her life that Johnson joined her for the voyage he describes. Subsequently, in 1932, she was sold to the British Shaftesbury Homes to replace the training ship *Arethusa* which had been in use since 1874. She was re-named *Arethusa* and moored in the Medway.

In 1939 she was loaned to the Royal Navy for use as accommodation for sailors and was re-named H.M.S. *Peking*. After the war, she reverted to her role as a cadet training ship until, in 1974, the school was moved ashore and the *Peking* was sold by auction to J Aaron Charitable Foundation of New York. She left the Medway in March 1975 and moved to Blackwall for work to be done to enable her to be towed across the Atlantic. Leaving England in July 1975, she reached New York after a passage of seventeen days. She has now been restored to her original state, with masts and yards replaced, and can be seen at South Street Seaport, New York.

Captain Jurs of Hamburg, who had already made more than fifty voyages round the Horn under sail, commanded the *Peking* when Johnson and his friend joined her as 'working passengers' in 1929. He made a great and lasting impression on Johnson, himself later to become a Captain in sail. He was feared and respected by the seventy-four members of the crew. He was explosively positive and knew just what had to be done. 'There are only two ways of doing a job; my way and the wrong way.' Johnson said, 'He taught me to lean forward into life'. What follows is Johnson's journal of that voyage.

115

The young Irving Johnson standing on his head on top of a telegraph pole to overcome his fear of heights, near his home farm

THE VOYAGE OF THE *PEKING* FROM HAMBURG TO CHILE VIA CAPE HORN, 1929–30, by Captain Irving Johnson

HAMBURG AND THE NORTH SEA

Hamburg is one of the most important of European ports, and full of great ships from many countries. Among these was the largest sailing ship in the world, the *Peking*, on which we were to voyage more than 11,000 miles to Chile. She was moored a little way out in the harbour, and we went to her in a motor boat. She was 'a great big wagon'; her hull, masts, and yards were steel, and I never had seen rigging better cared for. We met the captain in his cabin the first time we were on the vessel. He was like his ship – big – had big hands and a big smile, in fact was big in every way.

The day of our first call on the captain we went back to shore in the boat of a company official. A sailor's sea bag lay in the bottom, and I asked, 'What's that bag?' The official replied, 'A lot of trouble – that's what it is. The sailor it belonged to dropped off the *Peking*'s rigging into the sea on her last voyage.' And Charlie said in a low voice for only me to hear, 'I'm glad I made my will'.

We had expected to share the crew's quarters, but those were full, and we were assigned to a room amidships that opened off the captain's dining saloon.

Our starting day was the last Friday in November 1929. It was cold and rain fell most of the time. Another fellow and I bent on the outer jib. To do that we had to get up near the shark's tail at the end of the jib boom which projected beyond the bowsprit. Every old sailor thinks that a shark's tail as a jib boom decoration on a sailing ship is a necessity. It brings fair winds, and if a new ship is sailing, the crew cut off the tail of the first shark they catch and nail it up in the accustomed place. Moreover, in doing this they always are careful to have the longest part of the tail

point upward, for that makes fair winds more certain.

The only sail we set was the inner jib, but all the yards were hauled around to catch the wind and help the tug along. In the middle of the afternoon, sixty-five miles from Hamburg, we anchored at Cuxhaven near the mouth of the river to add a lot of airplane gasoline to our cargo. The *Peking* was now loaded to

The foremast of the Peking; *the main mast was the height of a seventeen storey building*

117

capacity, or 'down to her marks', as the seamen say. The hull was painted black, and the masts were painted a buff tint. Buff is used so commonly on ships for the purpose, that it is the custom of the sea to speak of it as 'mast colour'. We had a general cargo of everything from a couple of hundred tons of coke to 150 porcelain toilets. The main deck at the lowest point was only five feet above water level. She was drawing twenty-four feet of water, and that was too much for her to make her best speed.

When we were once more under way I started on a journey up the main mast to the royal yard, which is above all others near the top of the mast. I kept on until I was on the royal yard. If I had gone up in a building, I would have been seventeen stories high. After a while I noticed far below me twenty or more sailors who were strung along a yard bending the mains'l. I climbed down, took the position next to the end, and did my best without any instruction. One of the sailors told me to cut a certain line while we were up there. I was proud of having a good, sharp knife handy, and I 'whips it out' and cut the line. The sailor must have made some mistake, for no sooner was the cutting done than down fell half the sail. There was considerable talk about that little operation, because the sail had to be hauled back into place and it weighed nearly a ton.

Before we reached the open sea we dropped anchor again. That was because of the old superstition the captain had about beginning his ocean voyage on Friday. He didn't write anything in his log book until Saturday. But as we were to find out later, fate was not to be fooled so easily.

At daylight the next morning the tug heaved aboard her towing cable, and we hauled up our anchor. After that it didn't take us long to get out into the North Sea. In order to go faster we set all our heads'ls and stays'ls and the upper and lower spankers. The greater part of our crew consisted of young fellows fitting themselves to become officers, and they had to pay to go on the *Peking* for this purpose. Any old shellback will tell you that the man who has served his time in sail is worth two of those who have been to sea only in steamers. We had fifty-four of these cadets, whose ages varied from fifteen to twenty-four years.

Besides the cadets there were five regular sailors, the captain and four mates, two cooks, a steward, sailmaker, carpenter, blacksmith, bo'son, radio operator, and Charlie and me, making a total of seventy-four. Radio was a part of our equipment, but it would hardly send messages more than a hundred miles even under good conditions.

The *Peking* certainly was a big thing to be pushed around by the wind, but she had masts and yards that were proportionately as tremendous as she was. Our three royals, the highest sails on the ship, were over 175 feet above the water, and each of the three lower yards was one hundred feet long. 345 feet was the ship's length overall, her width was forty-seven feet, and her cargo load 4,700 tons. Among the voyagers on board were about a dozen hens, three pigs, and a turkey gobbler. The pigs had a built-in steel pen just aft of the foc'sle head.

During our first day on the North Sea I found time to go to the top of each of the four masts. Some of the ratlines were broken. They are used like the rungs of a ladder to put your feet on while climbing up and down, but a sailor never trusts them. He holds on to the shrouds at the side. We bent the last square sail that afternoon. Sailors call it the cro'jack, but dictionaries spell it crossjack. The decks were given a good scrubbing, harbour gear was put away, and sailing gear was gotten out. That was the ship's first washdown after over a month in dirty ports, and she looked much better afterward.

The crew had very crowded quarters, but we had the dining saloon to ourselves all the evening except for the captain's passing through occasionally. Sometimes he said a few words. One of his parting shots was, 'Ach Writing! And when you get back home you vill write a book with a lot of lies in it!'

The crew of the Peking, *seventy-four in all;*
two-thirds were cadets aged between fifteen and twenty-four

Sunday morning we set all sails except the royals and cro'jack. To do this, six great steel yards had to be hoisted twenty feet up the masts so the sails could be set under them. The hoisting of each yard was done by about eight men heaving on the iron cranks of a halyard winch for nearly half an hour.

At noon off the Hook of Holland the tug was let go, and she circled around astern to get our letters. Then she blew three blasts on her whistle, to which we responded with three blasts of our fog horn; and we gave three cheers which brought answering cheers from the tug crew. She could have continued the tow, but if we had a favourable wind a two-days' voyage would put us well past Dover where we would have no further need of a tug, and the owners of the *Peking* wanted to economise. We lay becalmed for several hours, and then picked up a north-northwest slant that sent us briskly along toward the English Channel.

The sailmaker and I became friends that day. Most of his forty or fifty years had been spent at sea where his experiences included all kinds of long voyages, storms, and shipwrecks. He told about a sailor's falling overboard on the last voyage of the *Peking*. A lifeboat was launched, but couldn't find a trace of the poor fellow. In 1911 the ship he was on started

119

Friday and was wrecked a few days later. Another Friday start on a voyage was made in 1924. It caused a broken rudder. After that had been fixed, the ship hadn't gone far when along came a worse storm and wrecked her. He didn't think that the vessel's stop overnight at the mouth of the Elbe would change the day of our start. 'It was on a Friday', he said, 'dot we left our port, Hamburg, and whether dot was in der captain's log or not will make no difference. Remember vot I say. I haf had experiences. We will be shipwrecked.'

Next morning the wind gradually got stronger until at eleven in the morning it was coming with a rush. We were diving into quite a sea and taking water over forward and aft. I went aloft to help with the sails. As I slid out on the foot rope, bending over between the to'gans'l yards, some inexperienced hand on deck let go the weather upper to'gans'l brace, and the huge steel yard came crunching down on my back with every roll of the ship. It crushed me until I thought I would pop with the pressure. The rest of the fellows set up a great holler until the yard was steadied. More sailors came out on the yard then and we finished furling the sail.

When hauling around the big fores'l it got to slatting because some one at the foc'sle capstan let the

Captain Irving Johnson, on board the Peking, *holding a salt cod waiting to be soaked for cooking. Next to him is his friend Charlie*

120

tack go too soon. About ten men gripped the capstan bars and began pushing around to take in on the sheet. That would save the sail if they worked fast enough. A capstan naturally is slow, but with the captain yelling his head off, and the mate cracking on the back or head, each man heaving at the bars, they whirled in a way that would have made a merry-go-round dizzy. The mate said we were having regular North Sea weather – by which was meant a south-west gale with rain-squalls, and short, steep, high seas. This was our first really rough weather, and several of the new boys turned green around the gills and had to lean over the lee rail.

In the night the wind blew itself out, and Tuesday opened with a smooth sea and a light southerly wind. The three pigs were allowed to run about the fore deck, and the poultry were let out aft. One very lively member of the ship's family was Mauritz, the cap-tain's short-haired, tan and white, mongrel dog. He did his best to bite the pigs, but he couldn't get a good hold. They ran to get away from him and made such a racket with their squealing that they roused every-body on board.

Every morning, so far, our breakfast fare had been steak and plenty of bread, butter, cold meats and cheese. At noon there was soup, and the soup-bone was served besides, so that we could whack off with a knife whatever hunks of meat still clung to it. The crew had the same variety in food that we had, but the amount they were served was limited. Down in the store-room were 320 bushels of potatoes, and enough other provisions for nine months.

The currents in the North Sea are very irregular, and a change of wind often shifts them from their normal direction. As a result we seldom knew just where we were. Two of the mates spoke English pretty well, and all of the cadets had studied it from three to six years, but only four or five could speak it. I started my German education by learning the names for our thirty-two sails. That was some job, but easy compared with learning the names later of the more

than 350 lines used in handling the sails. Those lines all had to be known by the feel, so that in a squall during a pitch black night we wouldn't let go the wrong one.

We got down past Dover some hours before day-light on the morning of 4 December, and only three miles more would put us past the end of a shoal into a broader part of the English Channel. But the wind changed, and we were obliged to go back into the North Sea. We shortened down to lower tops'ls and the fores'l while running north out of the Channel. The only thing we could do was to tack around in the North Sea until the wind became favourable again. This has been known to take weeks – and the weather report for the next day was southwest gales. Our fresh meat was all gone, and that pleased the captain because he liked the good old salt horse better.

Sure enough, the gales came the next day, and they were from the southwest, which was the course we wanted to steer. Friday was a fine clear day, but with a strong southwest wind that didn't do us any good. We were driven a long way north, and that night there was another gale. We had a regular 'he-man's' gale Saturday. I went up the foremast to help make fast the upper tops'l which had worked loose.

One of the men didn't steer well, and the captain took a poke at his jaw to encourage him to do better. But the poke missed the mark, and the captain's other big fist bent the fellow up by hitting him in the stomach. The captain was a whole show when he was mad – yelling, cursing, stamping the deck, and waving his arms. If ever there was a real, husky old sea-dog, he was one, standing six feet and two inches, weight 240 pounds, hands the largest I ever have seen, and his thumb nearly two inches wide. Except for a small moustache and goatee, he was clean shaven.

Sunday came with moderate southwest gales and some heavy squalls. In one of these squalls the mizzen topmast stays'l halyard parted, and before it could be taken in the sail was blown to shreds. The large seas got quite playful at times. There was one that lifted a

Catting the anchors

three-ton anchor which was catted over the bow. At once the mate and several sailors hurried to put on more rope and wire lashings, and there was no hesitation, though they knew that death would come to all of them, if while at their task there came another wave such as had jumped the 6,000 pound anchor.

The captain opened the slop chest as was the custom on Sunday. 'Slops' are all kinds of working-clothes, knives, pipes, tobacco and other small stores, and the crew bought eagerly. When the captain got tired of handing out the merchandise he closed the chest and said there would be no more sold until next week. Those who hadn't had a chance to buy were out of luck, and one of them started to protest, but the captain yelled, 'Raus!' That meant 'Get out', and it caused more action than any other word I ever had heard.

The sailmaker said that starting Friday on this voyage was the cause of all the gales that had assailed us. 'This ship never will get back to Hamburg,' he declared with great seriousness.

So much water came on deck Sunday night that one of the pigs was drowned, and in the morning some of the crew heaved the carcass overboard. Just after dark there was a great bang forward. The foretopmast headstay had parted! To have such a thing as that happen in a storm made it not unlikely that we would lose all our masts. Rain was falling and the night was pitch black. We couldn't see ten feet.

Once the ship made a dive that carried under water every man on the jib boom, and the whole lot of us came near being washed off at one swipe. It was great sport just the same out on that long jib boom, being given a wild ride by the plunging ship. When we took our noon sights the next day we found that after having drifted and sailed around on the North Sea for ten days, we were ten miles back of where the tug left us.

Our clothes didn't dry out unless we went to bed with them on, but even drying them like that was worthwhile because it was a great comfort in the morning to at least have dry clothes next to the skin.

Tuesday night, for the first time in more than a week, we were on the proper course for two hours. Our second mate frequently shook his head over the foolhardiness of the *Peking*'s starting the voyage on Friday. It looked as if he were right, didn't it? But nothing affected the keenness of our appetite on Friday or any other day. Everything went, from raw herring to lard on our bread instead of butter.

Thursday morning the wind was blowing in great shape. These German skippers hang onto sail just as long as possible, and that makes much harder the task of taking it in. The gale kept increasing, and in the afternoon those North Sea waves were the biggest the captain ever had seen there. What else could we expect? This was our thirteenth day out of Hamburg. We were off Amsterdam that Thursday afternoon with a real west-northwest full gale blowing. This placed us on a very bad lee shore, and we couldn't do a thing to help ourselves in the tremendous seas that were driving us toward the land.

The captain thought he would try to anchor, but on inspection we found that the violent waves had heaved the two anchors up from where they were catted at the bow, and hooked them into the deck. We might as well have had no anchors at all. A call was sent out for tugs by radio, but they wouldn't come except for salvage money. The storm was con-

tinually getting worse, and all the time the ship drifted toward land. I had been watching the storm from one place and another since eight o'clock in the morning, and what a wild and glorious sight it was – both beautiful and terrifying! This was the kind of storm I had wished for at the Giant's Causeway.

About midnight the captain radioed to the tugs to have them come anyway. I was in the chart room with him when the wireless operator came from his shack with their reply. The captain, after reading it, said, 'Vell, dose tugs can't come. Der storm is too bad. If dis keeps up ve vill be driven ashore about six in der morning.' Friday the thirteenth had begun, and didn't we start on a Friday? So the captain was almost certain that our fate was sealed.

Before I left the chart room I looked into the log book and saw that the captain had made a midnight entry estimating that the strength of the wind since six o'clock had been at force twelve, the highest rating in the Beaufort Scale, which describes Number Twelve as a hurricane. I went to my bunk and let the skipper do the worrying. I slept well until about four o'clock, when I woke up with a queer feeling that something was wrong. The motion of the ship wasn't as it should be. She was rolling and pitching around as if she were in a ground swell near shore.

On deck, I didn't dare speak to the skipper. He had been without sleep for three days and nights. All his thought was for the ship. I spoke to the mate. 'We've been drifting closer to land all the time,' he told me, 'and if there isn't a change pretty quick, we'll be wrecked all right.' A half hour or so passed and then unexpectedly, the wind began to moderate and to shift gradually to the southwest. Commands came thick and fast, and all hands jumped to the braces to wear ship.

Slowly she swung, heading more and more toward the land, because she only could swing her bow away from the wind; we could see the tremendous, foaming, phosphorescent breakers crashing over a reef between us and the lights on shore. The *Peking* takes

Some of the 350 lines for which the German names had to be learned

between two and three miles to turn in, and there was scarcely more than a three-mile space between us and the reef. Closer and closer she ran turning so slowly that we had to watch the compass to make sure she was swinging at all. She kept turning, and finally we were headed out into the North Sea. Then, by cracking on a lot of sail, we managed to get away from the coast.

Then the wind went down to a moderate south-westerly, which didn't do us much good, for there we were facing a head wind once more. I said to Charlie, 'Perhaps we will be North Sea pilots before we get out of here'. Saturday we were exactly where we had been the previous Saturday. We had fine sailing all day beating down in the general direction of Dover. It was a great sight to see the *Peking* come about. When a ship of this size comes about in a fresh breeze, your first impulse is to jump right overboard. You can't imagine that the long heavy steel yards could swing so fast without breaking off and coming down on your head.

When we took our Sunday sights we were within a few miles of our noon position twelve days before. The owners sent out a tug and the tug captain reported that in the worst storm of the series that had assailed us, sixty-nine ships had been wrecked. Not for half a century had there been so bad a storm in these waters.

NORTH SEA TO SOUTH ATLANTIC

Early on Monday, 16 December, we let the tug go. Then for the first time we set all sail including the royals and the spanker gaff tops'l. This made a total of thirty-one sails, and the *Peking* was a wonderful sight. She now had more than an acre of canvas spread to the light northwesterly breeze which shoved us along eight knots. About noon a lingering haze lifted and gave us a look at the Isle of Wight.

The captain knocked thunder out of two or three boys who didn't steer properly. One he slapped with his slipper. A boy who was looking on with me at a slipper-slapping said, 'Ven I see zee capatan, I travel a beeg circle so I vill not meet him'.

Everybody was busy on board after the North Sea gale. The galley stovepipe, which in all vessels is called Charlie Noble, for some unknown reason, was getting rusty and was given a coat of paint, and much of the wire rigging was greased down. Wednesday we were on the port tack making about seven knots with twenty-nine sails set. We had the Lizard abeam at noon.

Our second mate was only twenty-five, but he had a captain's ticket. One day he put the skipper's dog in the pen with the pigs. He was so full of mischief he just couldn't help entertaining himself in that way.

One of the things we had rather often for dinner was sweet raisin soup. We would find all kinds of things in our food, rotten peas and sturdy looking bugs in the pea soup. Sometimes we were served a prune soup, with dough balls that would do good service as sinkers for fishing in a strong current.

The captain's mongrel dog was about as mean tempered as they make 'em, and one day he bit a boy so badly that the captain had to attend to the wound. When the dog showed up in the cabin later, the captain grabbed him by the neck with his great hand, slapped him, and threw him out of the door.

There must have been a heavy gale somewhere in the North Atlantic, because we now started jumping into a big swell. Several experienced hands were sent aloft to furl the royals. They started work just as the ship took a deep dive. The yard went forward with a snap that tore the fellow beside me right off the yard. Down he went. Hardly had this happened when a wave under the bow brought the yard back just as quickly as it had gone. The fellow who dropped saw it returning just in time to catch hold of the foot rope where he had been standing, and soon he had pulled himself up on the yard, where with a smile at me, he went on furling the royal. That is what experience on a sailing ship teaches, 'Work for the ship while there is life left in your body'.

It was now three weeks since we left the Elbe, and we hadn't had a good breeze aft. Sunday night we passed a steamer that couldn't make anything like the *Peking*'s speed in the big sea which both were wallowing in.

Christmas was at hand. The Germans make a great deal of it, and the ship owners had provided five Christmas trees and plenty of trimmings for them — also apples, nuts, dried bananas, and cookies for everyone on board. I helped count and divide the stuff, including 2,000 cookies. The night before Christmas is the time the Germans celebrate most, although they have Christmas and the day after for legal holidays. Two of the boys had violins and two had accordions. They played very well, and the other boys all sang. There was something about the bunch of boys that evening, and the occasion, which made me catch my breath. They were in a sort of trance thinking of home and things far off in their native land.

The captain was superstitious about whistling. He thought it was a bad-weather breeder, and that it might cause the wrecking of the ship. He yanked a handful of hair out of the head of one boy who was whistling, and made him do penance for two hours on the royal. Christmas Day was the first one of the voyage when we could not dry our clothes except by going to bed with them on.

The ship's orchestra with their instruments, many of them home-made

A fresh northeasterly breeze was behind us on the 26th, and we had glorious sailing through clear, blue, sparkling water, with silver wave-tops. We passed the Canary Islands Friday morning at a distance of about twenty miles. The next evening we crossed the tropic of Cancer, and on ahead of us lay over 3,000 miles of sailing in the tropics.

A sailing vessel takes the prize for hard usage of one's hands, especially when hauling on the lines and handling the sails, in cold weather. Our hands got badly cracked and cut. We couldn't wash very clean, fresh water was so scarce, and most of us had infected fingers or wrists.

New Year's Day was celebrated by omitting work. However, the mates gave the first trippers a rope chase. A mate would call out the name of some line, and the boys had to run to catch hold of that line. If they didn't go fast enough they got a kick, or a swat with a rope's end.

We had now fallen back on the hard black bread which was our standby, and we ate it in preference to white bread. It always was kept several weeks to harden after it was baked, so we wouldn't eat it too freely. A sailor took a piece of that black bread and hit a wooden door with the edge of it. Quite a dent was made in the door, but the bread wasn't damaged.

The *Peking* was getting into the doldrums – the listless strip of the Atlantic just north of the equator, which stretches across to Africa from nearly opposite the mouth of the Amazon. On two days we were slowed down to an average speed of scarcely more than a mile an hour. The *Peking*, on her preceding voyage, had slatted around in the doldrums for a fortnight before she could get through its two or three hundred miles width.

The captain, aided by the chief mate and carpenter, gave the dog a bath. It was a good show for the onlookers. After soaking him properly the captain nearly drowned him in a barrel of salt water. That roused the wrath of the dog, and when he was let loose there was a great scramble to get out of his way.

Since leaving the English Channel a regular feature of Sunday had been a rope chase for the first-trippers. When the mate with his stinging rope's end got tired of whacking them he sent them up to some line at the masthead while he rested his arm; and when he got tired of chasing them around the deck he would set the skipper's dog after them to keep them running.

There was practically no drinking on the *Peking*. Only once was any grog passed out. That was in a bad storm, and none but the older men got it. Our skipper drank wine, but made a single bottle last through the trip.

On 8 January we were in the south-east trade winds and had fair weather all day. We crossed the equator Thursday afternoon, and all the crew, except those cadets who were first trippers, were eager to have a visit from King Neptune. But the captain wouldn't allow the old fellow on board. He said that Neptune and his court were so rough, that they often made trouble which had to be settled in the courts after the ship got back to Germany.

We were only 150 miles due east from Pernambuco, Brazil, on Monday 13 January. I did a lot of necessary repairing on my one good suit and then sponged it off. We had made fast time since leaving the Lizard, in spite of being slowed down a few days in the doldrums. There was some prospect of our overcoming even the handicap of being held so long buffetted by the gales in the North Sea.

Off Argentina the hatch tarpaulins were removed, and the hatch covers calked with oakum in preparation for Cape Horn. The captain figured how many voyages he had made around the Cape. The one he was making was his fifty-second.

At noon on Friday, the 16th, we were almost vertically under the sun. Our shadows were gone and even the big sails cast none worth mentioning. The wooden deck got too hot to stand on with bare feet, and we either wore shoes, or made quick runs from one narrow shadow to another, pausing on each in turn.

20 January the weather changed to a cool rain with a variable wind. The following morning a six-foot shark was caught, and the sailors cut out the big liver and let the sun dry out the oil. This they would use later to rub on their hands. The captain claimed it was the best ointment in the world to keep cold, wet, and stiff hands from cracking. One boy saved the flippers, another the tail, another the jaws and teeth, and still another treasured the pupils of the eye which would harden like rock and make good cuff links.

Saturday we made nearly twelve knots for the whole day, that is, 281 miles, the longest noon to noon run on the voyage. Few freighters can beat that. We were off the mouth of the River Plate – a vicinity noted for storms.

Wednesday, the 29th, we made fourteen knots from eight to nine in the morning. This was a lucky day because of the feed we got at noon. I had all the turkey, potatoes, gravy, and canned greens I could eat. On top of that I jammed three fourths of a prune pie. The chance wouldn't have come when it did if the turkey hadn't got sick. What a surprise – another feast next day! This time a sick hen had been discovered.

We stretched the new cro'jack along the deck and seized on the reef rope. It was a tremendous sail, and we had been twenty-eight days making it. An average of four men had worked on the job eight hours a day. We estimated that the sail weighed nearly a ton.

CAPE HORN

From latitude fifty on the east of South America to latitude fifty on the West is called 'the Horn', and mariners always figure from these points the number of days around. The distance as we planned to sail, going south of the Strait of Magellan and well away from the coast, was nearly a thousand miles.

That morning we had what the captain called 'American hash'. He said, 'I think dot I vill not eat any this time, there is too much of fresh meat in dot hash'. When we finished, the captain said, 'Vas dot good?' Just then the cook came in and asked him to dress his finger again, and we learned that while grinding the hash meat, the end of one finger had been taken off by the grinder. 'You two fellers vas cannibals,' he said, and he laughed at us for the next two weeks.

Sunday, the 9th, the wish that I first made at the Giant's Causeway came true. A real storm got started that morning and gathered headway all day. What I saw while the storm lasted can't be told in words. The log book showed a Number Twelve hurricane, long before the worst came. The blowing spray and flying spume turned the surface of the ocean white, except for faint greyish streaks, and the water around the ship and as far away as I could see had the appearance of being blanketed with snow. I always had wanted to see a big, heavy sail blow away in a hurricane, and now came my chance. The steel wire three quarters of an inch in diameter around the edge of the main lower tops'l broke with a noise that made me think some one had shot off a cannon. The canvas was the very heaviest made, and brand new, so it didn't all go at once, but banged and snapped making a racket like a machine gun.

A lone sailor went out to the end of the yard to let go the preventer sheet. If that banging sail had hit him once, it would have killed him. But he succeeded in letting go the sheet. Then a score of other sailors climbed up and joined him, and they furled what was left of the sail.

Later while the captain and I were eating dinner there was a jarring crash that felt and sounded like hitting a rock. On deck we found that a terrific wave had struck the port side of the ship and inspection revealed that a whole section of the side of the ship, twenty feet across, was bent in, steel plates, frames, and all. The skipper said he never had heard of a wave bending in the side of such a ship before.

I thought I would go up to the main royal yard to see if I could hold on under such conditions. When I had gone about to the height of the upper top'sl yard, a sea smashed against the windward side of the ship and sent spray over my head. It takes some force to shoot water up that high against such a gale. Meanwhile the sun occasionally shone down on all the confusion and violence and made dainty rainbows in the flying scud. As I neared the top of the mast I would stop whenever the ship rolled to windward, because I had such difficulty in pulling my feet back against the wind and getting them up to the next ratline. The air rushed past me at about 150 miles an hour, making a horrible screeching howl such as I never had heard before. The top of the mast swung in an arc fully 300 feet at some of the rolls, and these rolls of forty-five degrees often were made in eleven seconds.

I had demonstrated to myself that it was possible to hold on, and I went down, got my movie camera, and returned to the mast-top. After tangling my arms and legs up in the ratlines to keep from blowing away, I took movies of the Cape Horn grey backs that went sweeping across the deck of the ship 175 feet below me.

At noon on Monday we had been driven back eighty-four miles since the previous noon. One thing

The waves beginning to rise off Cape Horn

we lost in the storm was our shark's tail at the tip of the jib boom. Monday night we had eight sails set, as there was far less wind and the waves were smaller. There was a snow-squall in the afternoon, and when it was over we had a snowball fight. Cape Horn snow doesn't fall in flakes, but in little pellets like hail. It is known as Cape Horn sugar. We saw Cape Horn Tuesday morning. It rises abruptly to a height of 1,400 feet to it can be seen forty miles on a clear day. We were lucky to see it at all, for most ships go around the Horn without getting a sight of land. This was the first we had seen since passing the Isle of Wight about two months before.

There were head winds nearly all the time for several days, so that on Wednesday we were only ten miles from where we had been Sunday noon. A peach of a storm came up during the night. It was even better than the one on Sunday! According to the captain, the wind scarcely ever blows any harder. Summer storms, he claimed, were shorter, but stronger, than those in winter. I had a good time getting thrills out of the storms. There was charm in all the sights and sounds, and in the ever-varying motions of the vessel, the waves, and the clouds. A few weeks more battling in those savage waters at the Horn would have suited me.

In that second rip-snorter our barometer went down to 28.19 inches, which is the lowest sea level

Captain Johnson with a fish spear out on the bowsprit after Bonito

pressure I ever had seen or that I ever expect to see. Two years before our trip, the *Peking* made a voyage from Chile to Hamburg in seventy-seven days, and never took in a sail during all that time – an amazing record and how different from ours!

It was calm for a while on the morning of the 15th, but the swell from the previous day's storm hadn't smoothed out and we rolled in fine style.

The captain had two boxes of flowers under the skylight that was over the dining-room table. Each box was about four feet long, zinc-lined, and painted green. The captain himself watered and took care of the flowers. On our way down through the Atlantic the heat and sunshine encouraged them to unfurl their greenery and put forth some scattering blossoms. While we were rounding the Horn the skylights were shut, and the plants got no light to speak of. Now we were in gentler surroundings and the skipper opened the skylights. I happened to be standing close by at the time, and he turned to me exclaiming, 'Mine gracious! Look at dot. Der flowers are all dead.' Yes, and they were a melancholy sight. I was sorry for him.

After rounding the Horn and coming safely through the storms, we were interested in looking at the chart which showed our zigzag course when we were trying to beat against the westerly gales. Monday the 20th we were 135 miles from shore with a wind that would allow us to sail parallel with the almost straight north and south line of the coast of Chile. But the captain figured that we didn't have enough sea room. So he headed sou'sou'west back toward the latitudes of Cape Horn.

Since leaving Hamburg, Mauritz, the captain's dog, had taken a piece out of all but one of the officers and half the crew. The second mate, who teased him most, had escaped until now, when he got two holes through each of three fingers. The captain thought this was a great joke and spoke kindly to the dog.

One of the boys with a bad boil came to the captain's cabin for treatment, and the captain, as a part of his curative efforts, cut down to the bone and then squeezed the boil so hard that a sudden spurt of pus and blood flew fifteen feet up in the skylight. He sometimes used all the strength of his great arms in the boil-pinching.

On 21 February we completed the rounding of Cape Horn – a nineteen days' voyage. Rather slow, but ships have been known to take two months. Our noon sights the next day showed that only 450 miles lay between us and port. The ship, with the whole crew shining brass or painting, was beginning to look like a yacht. On Wednesday we were ninety days out, and we wondered what had happened in the world since we left it.

Friday the captain began to talk about the prospect of sighting land soon. So just after figuring out our noon position, I went up to the main royal taking along the skipper's binoculars. It was a fine, clear day, and sure enough there was land, although not much more than a blur. I shouted down, 'Land O, two points forward of the starboard beam'. This was a big event, and shore clothes began to be hung out to air.

Saturday morning, 1 March, we were just outside of Talcahuano harbour, about three hundred miles south of Valparaiso. A little tug came to take our towline, but instead, the captain arranged to have her take me for a little trip circling around to get moving pictures of the *Peking* under full sail. Then we took the towline, and with the almost negligible help of the tug, which had a big smokestack and a loud whistle, but no power, we beat our way up to the anchorage. There we made lively work of taking in sail while rounding up to drop our anchor about a mile from the town.

Charlie and I hadn't a cent to our names, but we borrowed some money from the captain. Then, each with a sea bag and suitcase, and Charlie with a knapsack besides, we went down the gangway and stepped into the harbour master's little motor boat

The Home of the Blizzard

'At the Southern Extremity of the Globe there is a vast unknown region. In the great span of 2,000 miles of Antarctic coast between Cape Adare and Gaus Berg, no land exploration has been undertaken. This virgin field is our goal.' Thus Sir Douglas Mawson, a noted Antarctic explorer of the time and the leader of the expedition, outlined his objective.

Yet this was to be primarily a scientific project; there was to be no attempt on the South Pole, still unreached at this time, though both Scott's and Amundsen's expeditions would actually get there while Mawson was in Antarctica.

Rather, Mawson planned a comprehensive scientific survey, extending over two Antarctic 'summers' and one 'winter' – the seasons being reversed at the South Pole with the 'summer' starting in October, the 'winter' in April. To achieve all his aims his ship, the *Aurora*, would put one group of scientist/explorers ashore on Macquarie Island, half-way between Australia and Antarctica; then she would land two more groups on the 'supposed continent' – Mawson's words, for the concept of a complete 'Antarctic continent' was still open to confirmation. *Aurora* would also carry out a programme of marine biology and underwater survey, which on 12 March, 1912 would take her to Hobart, Tasmania where she 'passed the Polar ship *Fram* at anchor: flags were dipped and a hearty cheer given for Captain Amundsen and his gallant comrades just returned from the South Pole'.

Mawson himself would be in charge of the larger of the two groups of scientists, the Main Base in Adelie Land. Here his team was to consist of eighteen souls, including cartographers, biologists, geologists, meteorologists, magneticians, astronomers, and a surgeon, among others. Landing on an unexplored coast, their wide-ranging discoveries in all fields were, again in Mawson's words, 'to prove unusually absorbing'.

Scientists or not, no one can escape adventure in Antarctica; and Mawson and his colleagues were to be called on to show courage and heroism on a scale that equals that of Scott or Shackleton. Perhaps because his expedition was primarily scientific, and fell between the achievements of two of the other 'greats' of polar exploration, Mawson is comparatively unknown. But the account by Sir Douglas Mawson that now follows, 'The Home of the Blizzard' is a truly amazing chapter in the history of exploration; a story of warmth and humanity – and an epic of courage and endurance.

Sir Douglas Mawson, leader of the Australasian Antarctic expedition

133

AUSTRALASIAN ANTARCTIC EXPEDITION, 1911–14, by Sir Douglas Mawson

PLAN AND PREPARATION: THE VOYAGE

To secure a suitable vessel was a matter of fundamental importance. The primary consideration in a vessel built to navigate amid the ice is that the hull be very staunch, capable of driving into the pack. So a thick-walled timber vessel, with adequate stiffening in the framework, would meet the case. The construction being of wood imparts a certain elasticity, which is of great advantage in easing the shock of impacts with floating ice. The ordinary steel ship would be ripped on its first contact with the ice.

The *Aurora*, of the Newfoundland sealing fleet, was ultimately purchased. She was built in Dundee, and though by no means young was still in good condition and capable of buffeting with the pack for many a year. The hull was made of stout oak planks, sheathed with greenheart and lined with fir. The bow, fashioned on cut-away lines, was a mass of solid wood, armoured with steel plates. The principal dimensions were, length 165 feet, carrying capacity about 600 tons. The engines registered ninety-eight horse-power, driving at the rate of six to ten knots. The ship was square on the foremast and schooner rigged on the main and mizen masts.

Saturday 2 December, arrived, and then began our final leave-taking from Tasmania. 'God speed' messages were received from far and wide, and intercessory services were held in the cathedrals of Sydney and Hobart. We were greatly honoured at this time in receiving a message of kind wishes for success from Queen Alexandra and, at an earlier date, from His Majesty King George V. At 4 p.m. sharp the telegraph was rung for the engines and we glided out into the channel.

The piles of loose gear presented an indescribable scene of chaos. Butter to the extent of a couple of tons was accommodated chiefly on the roof of the main deck-house, where it was out of the way of the dogs; besides, there was room for tide-gauges, meteorological screens, and cases of fresh eggs and apples. Somebody happened to think of space unoccupied in the meteorological screens, and a few fowls were housed herein.

Onward with a dogged plunge pressed our laden ship. Home and the past were effaced in the shroud of darkness, and thought leapt to the beckoning South – to the 'dawn' of undiscovered lands. The wind increased from bad to worse, and great seas continued to rise until their culmination about 4 a.m. on the morning of 5 December, when one struck the bridge, carrying the starboard side clean away. The officer on watch had a narrow escape; fortunately he happened to be on the other side of the bridge at the time.

At noon on 27 December whales were spouting all round us. Albatrosses constantly hovered about. Already we were steaming through untravelled waters, and new discoveries might be expected at any moment. 'Ice on the starboard bow' – at 4 p.m. on 29 December the cry was raised. On the outskirts was a light brash which steadily gave place to a heavier variety. A swishing murmur like the wind in the tree-tops came from the great expanse. It was alabaster-white and through the small, separate chips was diffused a pale lilac colouration. The *Aurora* retreated to the open sea, and headed to the west in search of a break in the ice-front. The wind blew from the south-east, and, with sails set to assist the engines, rapid progress was made.

Towards midnight on 6 January a bay was entered. Here the land was so overwhelmed with ice that, even at sea-level, the rock was all but entirely hidden. Here was an ice-age in all earnestness. The full truth was to be ascertained by bitter experience, after spending a year on the spot. I was now anxious to find a suitable location for our main Antarctic land base.

Advancing towards the mainland, we observed a

The Aurora *reaches her destination amid the ice flows and penguins*

small inlet in the rocky coast, and towards it the boat was directed. We were soon inside a beautiful, miniature harbour completely land-locked. The sun shone gloriously in a blue sky as we stepped ashore on a charming ice-quay – the first to set foot on the Antarctic continent between Cape Adare and Gaussberg, a distance of about two thousand miles. I proceeded to make a tour of exploration. Close to the Boat Harbour, as we called it, was suitable ground for the erection of a hut.

During the ensuing days, unloading operations were very much interfered with by the recurrence of severe gales off the land, yet, thanks to the assiduous application of all, a great assortment of material was at length safely got ashore. Comprised among them was the following: twenty-three tons of coal briquettes, two complete living-huts, a magnetic observatory, and more than 2,000 packages of general supplies containing sufficient food for two years. This work was completed on the afternoon of 19 January.

135

FIRST DAYS IN THE HOME OF THE BLIZZARD

Half an hour after leaving the *Aurora*, on the evening of 19 January, the overcrowded whale-boat deposited its human freight on the ice-quay. The only shelter was a cluster of four tents, so the first consideration was the erection of a commodious living-hut. The design chosen comprised a single square room with pyramidal roof. The roof slopes continued beyond the walls on the three windward sides to form a veranda which was in turn enclosed by an outer wall. There were four windows in the roof, one on each side of the pyramid. We should thereby get light even though almost buried in snow.

On the morning of 20 January all were at work betimes. As we were securely isolated from trade-union regulations, our hours of labour ranged from 7 a.m. to 11 p.m. Dynamite was to be used for blasting out the holes. When frozen, dynamite is not readily exploded. This was overcome by carrying the sticks inside one's pocket until the last moment. In the absence of earth or clay, we had no tamping material until someone suggested guano from the penguin rookeries, which proved a great success. We worked hard, ate heartily and enjoyed life.

The enthusiasm of the builders rose to its highest pitch as the roof neared completion, and we came in sight of a firm and solid habitation, secure from the winds which harassed us daily. A dozen hammers worked at once, each concentrated upon a specific job. The men inside nailing on the ceiling boards worked steadily ahead without interruption; the behaviour of those sitting on the roof busy on the outer covering was more erratic, as individuals were sometimes observed to start up suddenly and temporarily lose interest in the work.

On 30 January the main building was almost completed, and all slept under its roof. Bunks had been constructed, forming a double tier around three sides of the room. That night the sky, which had been clear for a fortnight, banked up with nimbus cloud and Murphy, who was sleeping under a gap in the roof, woke up next morning to find over him a thick counterpane of snow. Madigan was to take charge of the meteorological observations. Webb was engaged with the magnetic work.

It was now necessary to institute a routine of night-watchman, cooks and messmen. Regulations were drafted governing the issue of foods to the cook, and in the matter of meals we entered upon a routine. Breakfast was henceforth to consist of porridge followed by canned fruit. Lunch was made very appetising by a chief course selected from cold ham, fried sardines, salmon or other preserved fish. At dinner there was always soup, followed by penguin or seal in some form served with potatoes and a second preserved vegetable; finally a pudding course and a sweet dessert.

Our home had attained to a stage of complex perfection. The roof windows were immovable and soon became more securely sealed by a thick accumulation of ice on the inside. In the boarded floor of the porch was a trap-door which led down into a shallow cellar extending under the work-room.

The cellar was a natural refrigerating chamber for fresh meat, and contained fifteen carcases of mutton besides piles of seal meat and penguins. On account of the limited depth of this cellar it was an awkward job getting at the meat, necessitating a scramble on hands and knees with a wary look-out for projecting joists and stumps. Murphy, the storeman, who was rather ingenious in the matter of labour-saving devices, invented the plan of pushing a dog through the trap-door to bring out the penguins when required. As the dog sprang out Murphy would seize the bird, much to the disappointment of the dog. One fine day, however, the dog discovered one of the very few legs of mutton we possessed. Out he bounded and succeeded in evading Murphy who spent the greater part of an hour in pursuit. After this event the dog method was abolished.

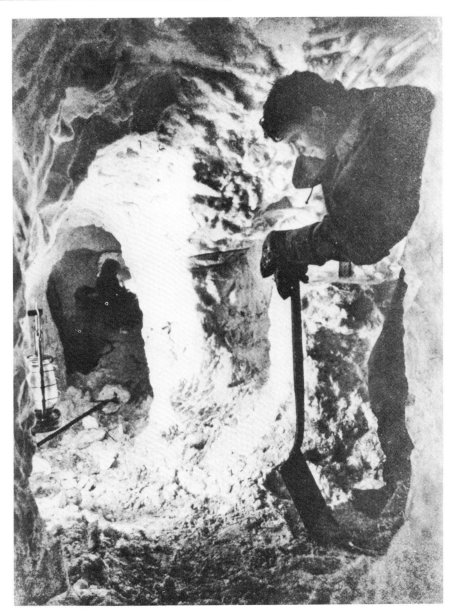

Digging out passages and catacombs around the snow-buried hut

Up to this date the dogs had been kept on the chain, on account of their depredations amongst the seals and penguins. Outside in heavy drift their habit was to take up a position in the lee of some large object, such as the Hut. In such a position they were soon completely buried and oblivious to the outside elements. Thus one would sometimes tread on a dog, hidden beneath the snow; and the dog often showed less surprise than the offending man. It was really wonderful that the dogs managed as well as they did in such conditions. One amusing habit was frequently observed whilst out walking with them in windy weather. No sooner would one halt for some purpose or another than all the dogs would squat down in a line, each in the lee of the other. As soon as number one realised he was being made a screen he got up and trotted round to the back. A moment later number two would follow him, and so on until in sheer disgust they would break up the formation.

The equinox arrived, and the only indication of settled weather was a more marked regularity in the winds. Nothing like it had been reported from any part of the world. Any trace of elation we may have felt at the meteorological discovery could not compensate for the discomforts of life. Day after day the wind fluctuated between a gale and a hurricane. Overcast skies and heavy nimbus clouds were the rule and the air was charged with drifting snow.

'The home of the blizzard': the hut in a snow squall. Winds of sixty and seventy miles an hour made walking upright impossible

THE BLIZZARD

The climate proved to be little more than one continuous blizzard the year round; a hurricane of wind roaring for weeks together, pausing for breath only at odd hours. Progression in a hurricane became a fine art. The first difficulty to be encountered was a smooth, slippery surface offering no grip for the feet. Stepping out of the shelter of the Hut, one was apt to be immediately hurled at full length down wind. No amount of exertion was of any avail. The strongest man, stepping on to ice or hard snow in plain leather or fur boots, would start sliding away with gradually increasing velocity; in the space of a few seconds or earlier, exchanging the vertical for the horizontal position. He would then either stop suddenly against a jutting point of ice, or glide along for twenty or thirty yards till he reached a patch of rocks. Some of the men covered the soles of their boots with long, bristling spikes and these served their purpose well. Spikes of less than an inch in length were inadequate in hurricanes. Before the art of 'hurricane-walking' was learnt, progression in high winds degenerated into crawling on hands and knees. Many of the more conservative persisted in this method.

Wind alone would not have been so bad; drift snow accompanied it in overwhelming amount. Day after day deluges of drift streamed past the Hut, at times so dense as to totally obscure objects three feet away, until it seemed as if the atmosphere were almost solid snow. Picture drift so dense that daylight comes through dully, though, maybe, the sun shines in a cloudless sky; the drift is hurled, screaming through space, at a hundred miles an hour, and the temperature is far below zero, Fahrenheit. You have then the bare, rough facts concerning the worst blizzards of Adelie Land. The actual experience of them is another thing.

It may well be imagined that none of us went out on these occasions for the pleasure of it. The scientific work required all too frequent journeys to the instruments at a distance from the Hut. The meteorological instruments, carefully nursed and housed though they were, were bound to suffer in such a climate. Correll, who was well fitted out with a lathe and all the requirements for instrument-making, attended to repairs, doing splendid service.

In thick drifts, one's face became rapidly packed with snow, which, by the warmth of the skin and breath, was converted into a mask of ice. This adhered firmly to the beard and face; though not particularly comfortable, it was actually a protection against the wind. The mask became so complete that one had continually to break it away in order to

*The ice-mask of the meteorologist, after
checking the instruments in a blizzard*

breathe and to clear away obstructions from the eyes. It frequently happened that the face was superficially frost-bitten beneath the mask, areas of hard white flesh showing up as the ice was removed. In the absence of a toilet mirror such patches, being devoid of feeling, were easily mistaken by the individual for an obstinate remnant of the ice mask. Thus it was that Madigan was once observed toying with a lifeless cheek endeavouring to remove it under the impression that it was ice.

The abrasion effects produced by the impact of the snow particles were astonishing. Rope was frayed, wood etched and metal polished. Some rusty dog-chains were exposed to it, and in a few days they had a definite sheen. A deal box, facing the wind, lost all its painted bands and in a fortnight was handsomely marked; the hard knotty fibres being only slightly attacked, whilst the softer, pithy laminae were corroded to a depth of one-eighth of an inch.

The snow continued to descend in torrents and, but for the wind, the Hut would have been quite lost to sight. The packed drifts rose higher and higher round the walls, and back eddies brought the snow past the canvas flap at the entrance, though situated on the lee side, until the veranda became choked. Frequent shovelling was necessary to maintain freedom of exit.

At the inner extremity of the entrance tunnel, the roar of the tempest died away to a rumble, the trap-door opened and perhaps the strains of the gramophone would come in a kind of flippant defiance from the interior. Passing through the vestibule and workshop one beheld a scene in utter contrast to the outer hell. Here warm bunks, rest, food, light and companionship – for the time being – heaven.

There were several occasions in April when the velocity of the wind exceeded ninety miles an hour. On 11 May, the average for the twenty-four hours was eighty miles per hour. On 15 May, the wind blew at an average velocity of ninety miles per hour throughout the whole twenty-four hours.

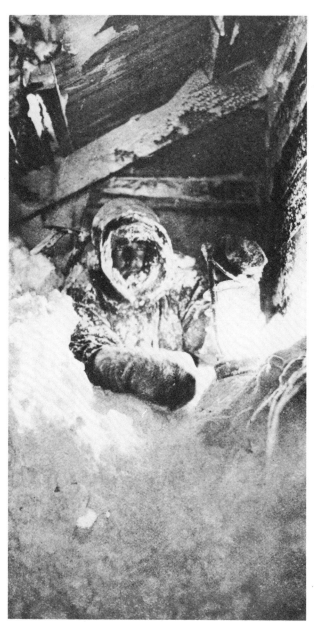

The nightwatchman on the snow-choked veranda of the hut

DOMESTIC LIFE

Our hearth and home was the living-hut, and its focus was the stove. Kitchen and stove were indissolubly linked. Around and above the stove hung oddments like fur mitts, finnesko, socks, stockings and helmets, which had passed from icy rigidity through sodden limpness to a state of parchment dryness. Those in charge of the culinary affairs viewed with great disfavour the surreptitious hanging of garments over the range, for these had a habit of dripping into the tea-water as they thawed, or of falling into the soup with a strong probability of imparting an undesirable bouquet of dog and blubber. So the problem was to recover one's own property and at the same time to avoid the cook engaged in scraping the porridge-saucepan and the messman scrubbing the table.

Birthdays were always greeted with special enthusiasm. Speeches were made, toasts were drunk,

Leisure time in the hut: a chance to read or play the gramophone

the supple boards of the table creaked with good things, cook and messman vied with each other in lavish hospitality. The Hut was ornate with flags, every man was spruce in his snowiest cardigan and neck cloth, the gramophone sang of music-hall days, the wind roared its appreciation through the stove-pipe, and rollicking merriment was supreme. Celebrations were carried on into the night, but no one forgot the cook and the messman. The table was cleared by many willing hands. The majority then repaired with pipes and cigars to 'Hyde Park Corner', where the storeman entertained the smoker's club. A mixed concert brought the evening to the grand finale – 'Auld Lang Syne'.

The mania for celebration became so great that in search of memorable occasions reference was frequently made to an almanac of notable events. So it happened that during one featureless interval, the anniversary of the 'First Lighting of London by Gas' was observed with extraordinary eclat.

Inside the hut's workshop: repairing meteorological instruments broken by the blizzard

The great medium of monetary exchange was chocolate. A ration of one cake totalling thirty squares was distributed by the storeman every Saturday night, and for purposes of betting, games of chance, 'Calcutta sweeps' on the monthly wind-velocity and general barter, chocolate held the premier place. As a consequence of wild speculation, there were several cases of bankruptcy, which was redeemed in the ordinary way by a sale of the debtor's effects.

While the wind rushed by at a maddening pace and stars flashed like jewels in a black sky, a glow of pale yellow light overspread the north-east horizon – the aurora polaris. At times the light was nimble, flinging itself about in rich waves, warming to dazzling yellow-green and rose. These were the nights when 'curtains' hung festooned in the heavens, alive, rippling, dancing to the lilt of lightning music. Up from the horizon they would mount, forming a vortex overhead, soundless within the silence of the ether. A 'brilliant display', we would say, and the observer would be kept busy following the track of the evanescent rays. Powerless, one was in the spell of an all-enfolding wonder. The vast, solitary snow-land, cold-white under the sparkling star-gems; lustrous in the rays of the southern lights. We had come to probe its mystery, we had hoped to reduce it to terms of science, but there was always the 'indefinable' which held aloof, yet riveted our souls.

Throughout the winter, the preparation of sledging equipment was a standing job in which all participated as opportunity offered. In the matter of clothes for the Antarctic land parties, we were provided with abundance of thick woollen underclothing, and with outer garments of Jaeger fleece. An over-suit of wind-proof material, Burberry gaberdine, made to our own designs, was also supplied to be worn when necessary. For the extremities there were fur mitts made of wolf skin, as well as woollen ones; and, in addition to the usual heavy leather ski-boots, we had fur boots from Lapland (finnesko) of reindeer skin.

Scientific appliances were accumulated from divers sources. Finally there were fur sleeping-bags of reindeer skin, sledges from Norway, and Esquimaux dogs from Greenland.

In the matter of sledging foods, it is of prime importance to reduce as far as possible the weight of food taken upon any journey. Our allowance was made up as follows, the relative amounts in the daily sledging ration for one man being stated: biscuit, 12 oz; pemmican, 8 oz; butter, 2 oz; chocolate, 2 oz; glaxo (dried milk), 5 oz; sugar, 4 oz; cocoa, 1 oz; tea, 0.25 oz; a total of 34.25 oz. The pemmican consisted of powdered dried beef with an addition of 50 per cent of beef fat.

The hut was agog with movement and bustle on the days when rations were being made up and packed. The foods were taken out of tins, weighed out into weekly rations and prepared as far as possible to save operations while sledging. There was the hoosh-compound, a mixture of chopped up pemmican and crushed plasmon biscuit. The tea, in rations for a single brew, was sewn up in small muslin bags ready to be dropped into the cooker. Meanwhile, other occupations were in full swing.

SPRING EXPLOITS

It was not until 8 August that there was any indication of improvement in the weather. But on the 17th the wind was gauged at eighty-four miles an hour, and nothing could be done. Dense drift and ferocious wind continued until the morning of 21 August. October came with a deluge of snow and transient hours of bright sunlight, during which the seals would make a temporary landing. The first penguin of the Antarctic 'spring' came waddling up the ice-foot against a seventy-mile wind on the afternoon of 12 October. McLean brought the bird back to the Hut and the newcomer received a great ovation. The penguins were a never-failing source of interest and

A sledging party of the Australasian Antarctic expedition

amusement; it was quite an entertainment to spend half an hour amongst them in one of the many rookeries near by. These droll little fellows, pugnacious to a degree and altogether ignorant of man, have no fear but, on the contrary, approach resolutely pecking at one's legs or else, ignoring one entirely, go about their business undisturbed.

October closed with an average wind velocity of 56.9 miles per hour. Yet the possibility of summer sledging was no longer remote. The sun was high, spells of calm were longer and more frequent, and, with the certain knowledge that we should be on the plateau in November, the sledging parties were chosen, schemes of exploration were discussed, and the last details for an extensive campaign completed.

The following is a list of the parties which had been arranged and fully equipped: 1) A Southern Party; the special feature of their work was to make magnetic observations. 2) A Western Party who were to traverse the coastal highlands west of the Hut. 3) An Eastern Coastal Party. 4) Finally, a Far-Eastern Party, assisted by the dogs, was to push out rapidly overland, mapping more distant sections of the coast-line. As the plans for the execution of such a journey had of necessity to be more provisional than in the case of the others, I determined to undertake it myself, accompanied by Ninnis and Mertz, both of whom had so ably acquitted themselves throughout the expedition and, moreover, had always been in charge of the dogs.

November opened with more moderate weather, auguring still better conditions for midsummer. Accordingly 6 November was fixed as the date of final departure. Everybody was on the tiptoe of expectation. The evening of 5 November was made a special occasion: a farewell dinner, into which everybody entered very heartily. At this date the penguin rookeries were full of new-laid eggs, and the popular taste inclined towards omelettes, in the production of which we found Mertz was a past master. I can recall the clamouring throng that pressed round for the final omelette as Mertz officiated at the stove just before we left on the 10th.

It was a beautiful calm afternoon as the sledge mounted up the long icy slopes. With a view to avoiding crevasses as much as possible, a southerly course was followed for several miles. In the meantime the wind had arisen and snow commenced to fall, so after having covered eight miles we decided to camp and await a clearance in the weather. Operations connected with camping at the end of a day's march developed into a set routine. First the sledges are drawn across the wind where they serve as a break-wind to shelter the dogs. Snow blocks are broken out ready and then the tent itself is erected and made snug against the onslaught of the weather.

Whilst two of the party tether and feed the dogs, the cook of the occasion takes the food into the tent and prepares the meal. The primus is started and over it is placed the cooker filled with snow. Very soon into it is dumped a measured quantity of hoosh-compound. A few minutes more and it has reached the boil. The ration of biscuit is eaten with the cocoa and presently the meal is over. Then commences a general clean up with the object of removing all loose snow from the gear in the tent.

After this there is little left to do, for on sledging journeys one does not indulge in elaborate toilet arrangements, nor did we ever undress. However, before slipping down into the bag a complete change of footgear is made, donning warm dry sleeping socks. The damp socks are pushed under one's jacket where the heat of the body is relied upon to dry them by the morning. The more or less sodden finnesko are usually quite limp as they are removed from the feet but soon freeze stiff, so rigid that they cannot be drawn on to the feet in the morning unless care has been taken that in the freezing they retain the proper shape of the foot.

Returning to events of 11 November, five days of wind and drift followed. On such occasions, when weather-bound in our sleeping bags, we made it a

145

Exploring an ice cliff

practice to eat very little food, saving what we could for future emergencies. Outside the dogs had a very unpleasant time, but fortunately they were soon buried in snow which sheltered them from the stinging wind. On the morning of the 17th the dogs were in fine fettle, barking with joy, rushing the sledges along.

If the weather is reasonably good and food is ample, the dogs enjoy the work. Their desire to pull is doubtless inborn, implanted in a long line of ancestors who have faithfully served the Esquimaux. We found that they were glad to get their harnesses on and to be led away to the sledge. Indeed, it was often a case of the dog leading the man, for, as soon as the harness was in place, the impatient animal strained to drag whatever might be attached to the other end of the rope.

Before harnessing up a team of dogs, it was necessary to anchor the sledge firmly, otherwise in their ardour they would make off with it before everything was ready. There can be no question as to the supreme value of dogs as a means of traction in the polar regions. It is only in such special circumstances as when travelling continuously over very rugged country, over heavily crevassed areas, or during unusually bad weather that man-hauling is-to be preferred.

At 9.45 a.m. on 18 November everything was ready for a fresh start. It was a lovely day; almost like a dream after so many months of harassing blizzards.

The surface became softer and smoother as the afternoon lengthened until Mertz was tempted to put on his skis. As Mertz was exceptionally expert with them, it had been agreed that one pair should be included in the equipment. On occasions such as the present when the surface was suitable, Mertz would don his skis and relieve Ninnis and myself in the van. Ninnis developed a touch of snow-blindness which, however, rapidly improved under treatment. The stock cure for this very irritating and painful affliction is to place tiny tabloids of zinc sulphate and cocaine hydrochloride under the eyelids where they quickly dissolve in the tears, alleviating the smarting, gritty sensation. This operation is usually effected when retiring to the sleeping-bag, then the sufferer has an opportunity of keeping his eyes closed for some hours. In acute cases the eyes are bandaged.

We had now settled down to a definite order of march. Behind the forerunner came the first team of dogs dragging two sledges which were joined together by a short length of rope. Bringing up the rear were the rest of the dogs harnessed to the third sledge. I looked after the leading team; Ninnis or Mertz, as the case might be, driving the one behind. It was all smooth travelling that afternoon and over such a surface we expected to cover a long distance before halting for the day.

Suddenly without any warning the leading dogs of my team dropped out of sight, swinging on their harness ropes in a crevasse. The next moment I realised that the sledges were on a bridge covering a crevasse, twenty-five feet wide, the dogs having broken through on one edge. We spent some anxious moments before they were all hauled to the daylight and the sledges rested on solid ground.

The next morning opened with a chill wind blowing drift-snow down the glacier bed. Travelling was rather miserable, especially as crevasses lurked beneath the crust, some of them gaping wide open. Occasionally some of the dogs broke through, but without mishap. In the afternoon the weather cleared but, the broken surface became hopelessly shattered and tossed about. The region was one of serac ice where the glacier was puckered up, folded and crushed. We were finally forced to camp, having ten miles to our credit. On waking up on 24 November I found that my watch had stopped. I had been so tired on the previous evening that I had fallen asleep without remembering to wind it.

The tent was raised at 10 p.m. in a forty-mile wind with light drift. One of the worst features of drift overnight is that sledges and dogs become buried in snow and have to be dug out in the morning.

*One of the many ice cliffs and crevasses,
that in bad weather could swallow a sledge and team*

(For the next nineteen days the three men, Mawson, Ninnis and Mertz pressed on Eastwards: taking sights, making camp, avoiding glaciers, struggling through storms. 13 December found them some 300 miles from the Hut and on the point of turning for home.)

A light east-south-east wind was blowing as the sledges started away eastward on the morning of 14 December. The weather was sunny and the temperature registered 21°F. We were a happy party that morning as we revelled in the sunshine and laid plans for a final dash eastwards before turning our faces homewards. Mertz who was well in the lead, the conditions being both suitable and agreeable for employment of skis, was in high spirits as was evident from the snatches of song wafted back from time to time. I noticed Mertz halt for a moment and hold up his ski-stick – this was a signal that something unusual was afoot. Approaching the vicinity with the foremost sledge a few minutes later, I kept a look-out for crevasses or other explanation of his action. A moment later the faint indication of a crevasse passed beneath the sledge but it had no appearance of being in any degree specially dangerous. However, as had come to be the custom I called out a warning to Ninnis, who was close behind walking along by the side of his sledge. There was no sound from behind except a faint, plantive whine from one of the dogs which I imagined was in reply to a touch from Ninnis's whip.

When next I looked back, it was in response to the anxious gaze of Mertz who had turned round and halted in his tracks. Behind me nothing met the eye except my own sledge tracks running back in the distance. Where were Ninnis and his sledge? I hastened back along the trail thinking that a rise in the ground obscured the view. There was no such good fortune, however, for I came to a gaping hole in the surface about eleven feet wide. The lid of the crevasse that had caused me so little thought had broken in; two sledge tracks led up to it on the far side – only one continued beyond.

Frantically waving to Mertz to bring up my sledge, upon which there was some alpine rope, I leaned over and shouted into the dark depths below. No sound came back but the moaning of a dog, caught on a shelf just visible 150 feet below. The poor creature appeared to have a broken back, for it was attempting to sit up with the front part of its body, while the hinder portion lay limp. Another dog lay motionless by its side. Close by was what appeared in the gloom to be the remains of the tent and a canvas food tank containing a fortnight's supply. We broke back the edge of the hard snow lid and, secured by a rope, took turns leaning over, calling into the darkness in the hope that our companion might be still alive. For three hours we called unceasingly but no answer came back. The dog had ceased to moan and lay without a movement. A chill draught rose out of the abyss. We felt that there was no hope. It was difficult to realise that Ninnis, who was a young giant in build, so jovial and so real but a few minutes before, should thus have vanished without even a sound. It seemed so incredible that we half expected, on turning round, to find him standing there.

Why had the first sledge escaped? The explanation appeared to be that Ninnis had walked by the side of his sledge, whereas I had crossed it sitting on the sledge. The whole weight of a man's body bearing on his foot is a formidable load, and no doubt was sufficient to smash the arch of the roof. By means of a fishing line we ascertained that it was 150 feet sheer to the ledge upon which the remains were seen; on either side the crevasse descended into blackness. It seemed so very far down there, and we got out the field-glass to complete the scrutiny of the depths. All our available rope was tied together but the total length was insufficient to reach the ledge, and any idea of going below to investigate had to be abandoned.

At 9 p.m. we stood by the side of the crevasse and I read the burial service.

149

*Lt B. E. S. Ninnis of the Royal Fusiliers,
who lost his life in a crevasse*

TOIL AND TRIBULATION

The homeward track; a few days ago – only a few hours ago – our hearts had beaten hopefully at the prospect and there was no hint of this, the overwhelming tragedy. With regard to the dogs, there were but six very miserable ones left. The best animals had been drafted into the rear team, as it was expected that if an accident were to happen through the collapse of a crevasse lid the first sledge would in all probability be the sufferer.

For the same reason most of the food and other indispensable articles had been carried on the rear sledge. The whole of the dog food had been lost and there remained but a bare one and a half weeks' man-food. In addition, the tent with its floor-cloth and poles, the spade, ice-axe, mugs and spoons, and Mertz's burberry trousers were numbered among the missing. Fortunately, the spare tent-cover happened to have been on the first sledge and needed only some sort of a frame over which to spread it. Thus handicapped with the loss of these articles our return to the Hut, a journey of over 300 miles, was made so much more difficult.

A silent farewell, and we started back, aiming to reach our camping ground of 12 December, where several things had been discarded which should be of use in our straitened circumstances. All speed was necessary before snow should fall and obliterate the track which alone served to locate the goal. At half past two in the early morning of 15 December, the relics discarded at our camps of three days previous came into sight. Projecting from the snow were the remains of the damaged sledge and the broken spade. Two pannikins were produced, cut out of tins in which cartridges and matches had been packed; wooden spoons were carved out of the frame of the broken sledge.

There was no breeze that afternoon and a bright sun shone in the sky. We had already decided to march during the evening hours when the surface would be crisp, offering the best conditions for sledging. Camp was, therefore, not finally broken until 6 p.m. when the long and painful journey to the Hut commenced.

We plodded on hour after hour while the sun sank lower in the southern sky. For fourteen miles the way led up rising snow slopes. We banished thoughts of food as completely as possible, knowing well that nothing of that kind could be afforded to provide a welcome break in the day's march. Our daily work in future promised to be long and tedious with no prospect of refreshment until the final halt. At 6 a.m., having covered a distance of twenty miles, we pitched camp. The dogs were thoroughly exhausted.

Ours was a mournful procession as we moved off that evening; the sky thickly clouded, snow falling, I with one eye bandaged and the dog Johnson, whom we found too exhausted to walk, strapped on top of the load on the sledge. A snow-hush brooded over the scene. Beyond the dismal whining of Johnson, into whose body the frost was swiftly penetrating, there was scarcely a sound; only the rustle of the thick, soft snow as we pushed on. The dogs dumbly pressed forward in their harness, forlorn but eager to follow. Their weight now told little upon the sledge, the work mainly falling upon ourselves.

We were making about due west and it was a most difficult task in overcast calm weather to keep anything like a proper course. The magnetic compass was quite useless. So by 2 a.m. on the 17th, though only eleven miles had been covered, a halt was called. Poor Johnson was too weak to stand up or even to eat his ration of meat, so after he had fumbled about with it and licked it for some time we decided to finish him off, as it was quite certain that he would never again be strong enough to march. Johnson had always been a very faithful hard-working and willing beast, with rather droll ways of his own, and we were very sorry that his end should come so soon.

A fresh start was made at 7.30 p.m. and a

The great crumpled ice sheet of Antarctica . . .

wretched, trying night it proved, marching under adverse conditions without a break for twelve and a half hours. I could not have wished for a better companion in such adversity than Mertz. He was always full of life and vigour and his good spirits helped to make those trying days pass as cheerfully as possible. Each mile ticked off by the sledgemeter we recorded by a pencil mark on the tail-board of the sledge. In the early morning hours we came near to losing the dog Haldane, the big grey wolf, in a crevasse. Fortunately I was just able to grab a fold of his skin. Haldane took to the harness once more, but soon became uncertain in his footsteps, staggered along and then tottered and fell.

Poor brutes. That was the way they all finished up. From putting little or no weight into the harness they relapsed into an uncertain 'groggy' pace with a slack trace; a few miles more and they would commence to totter and stumble, soon to rise no more.

At 9 p.m. 21 December, the march was resumed in the face of a strong and chilly south-south-east wind accompanied by low drift. The dog Pavlova, who had already collapsed during the march of the previous day, had to be hoisted on to the sledge. The outlook was darkening, for the days brought us more than a reasonable share of bad weather; this combined with crevassed and awkward surfaces landed us in most undesirable circumstances.

Of the dogs there was only Ginger left; the pack had gone down in a way never to have been foreseen. This all showed how little nutriment there can have been in the carcases of their stricken fellows. Our own experience also bore this out, for our strength was decreasing in a way that indicated that the dog-meat was more filling than nutritious. However, about this time we discovered that we could afford to be more lavish with the kerosene and in future boiled the meat and bones in the cooker with much more satisfactory results.

So it came about that at that camp of 23 December we treated ourselves to what we deemed a delicious soup made from some of Pavlova's bones cracked open with the spade. Confined to camp until the weather cleared, we set to work to boil a supply of meat sufficient to last for several days. By long boiling the sinews and gristle were reduced to the consistency of jelly. The paws took longest to cook, but, treated to a lengthy stewing, even they became quite digestible.

At about 8 a.m. on 24 December the sun commenced to gleam through the clouds and we got under way as cheerily as possible. After four miles we were driven to halting until the evening, when it was expected that the surface would harden. We were up at 11 p.m., but so much time was absorbed in making a special stew for Christmas from some of the bones that it was not until 2.30 a.m. that we got under way. To make the spread more exceptional I produced two scraps of biscuit which I had saved up, stowed away in my spare kit-bag, as relic of the good days before the accident. It was certainly a cheerless Christmas; we wished each other happier anniversaries in the future, drinking the toast in dog soup.

After a run of eleven miles we commenced to raise the tent at 9.30 a.m. I took observations for position, computing the distance in an air-line to the Hut to be 160 miles. We had reached the half-way point on our return journey. At the meal an ounce each of butter was served out from our small stock to give a festive touch to the stew. There never was a trace of fat associated with any of our dog preparations and we positively longed for it.

The next morning, 26 December, we got under way at 2 a.m. The sun shone, but there was a strong, penetrating, chill wind reaching forty miles per hour and raising low drift. We found the march very trying and by noon, when camp was pitched, had covered little over ten miles.

At this time the ration was mainly composed of dog meat to which was added one or two ounces of chocolate or raisins, three or four ounces of a mixture of pemmican and biscuit, and, as a beverage, very dilute cocoa. In all the total weight of solid food consumed by each of us per day was about fourteen ounces. The small supply of butter and glaxo was saved for emergency, while a few tea bags that remained were each boiled over and over again. As we worked on a system which aimed at using up the bony parts of the carcase first, it happened that Ginger's skull figured as the dish for the next meal. As there was no instrument capable of dividing it, the skull was boiled whole and a line drawn round it for marking it into right and left halves, after which, passing the skull from one to the other, we took turns about in eating our respective shares. The brain was certainly the most appreciated and nutritious section, Mertz remarking specially upon it. Before retiring to the sleeping-bag, I spent another four hours cracking and boiling down bones with the object of extracting the nutriment for future use and at the same time

Preparing a meal in Antarctica

ridding the load of a lot of useless weight in the form of inert bone.

We were away at 2.30 a.m., 29 December, in a thirty-mile wind and light drift. In the latter part of the march I realised that my companion was not as cheerful as usual. On talking things over with Mertz, I found that he had found the dog meat very disagreeable and felt that he was getting little nutriment from it. He suggested that we should abstain for a time from eating any further of this meat and draw solely upon the ordinary food of which we still had some days' supply carefully husbanded. This plan was adopted as it was expected to act beneficially on our health. I will always remember the wonderful taste that the food had in those days. Acute hunger enhances the taste and smell of food beyond all ordinary conception. The flavour of food under such conditions is a miracle altogether unsuspected by the millions of mortals who daily eat their fill. Cocoa was almost intoxicating and even plain beef suet, such as we had in fragments in our hoosh mixture, had acquired a sweet and aromatic taste scarcely to be described.

Snow continued to fall all day long throughout New Year's day and the light remained as bad as ever. Mertz was not up to his usual form and had not responded to the change of diet. Later in the day Mertz lost appreciation of the biscuit; it was then that I first began to realise that something really serious was the matter and that his condition was worse than my own. As he expressed a desire for glaxo our small stock was made over to him, a larger proportion of biscuit and dog-meat falling to my share. The wretched conditions persisted on 2 January.

We longed for a good fine day when we could tramp on by the hour and appreciably lessen the distance ahead. At length in the evening of 3 January the clouds broke and the sun peered through for a time. We were not long in packing and getting on the way. It was an exceptionally cold night, and the wind pierced our emaciated frames like a knife. Alas, before five miles were covered we were again in camp for Mertz had suddenly developed dysentery. To make matters worse his fingers had been badly frostbitten, which for a moment he himself could scarcely believe, for so resistant to cold was he that he had never before suffered in this way. To convince himself he bit a considerable piece of the fleshy part off the end of one of them.

6 January was a great improvement on its predecessors, but the sky still remained overcast. Mertz agreed to try another stage. Falls were frequent and they soon told severely upon my companion in his weak condition. There was nothing to do but pitch the tent. Starvation combined with superficial frostbite, alternating with the damp conditions in the sleeping-bags, had by this time resulted in a wholesale peeling of the skin all over our bodies. As we never took off our clothes, the peelings of hair and skin from our bodies worked down into our under trousers and socks, and regular clearances were made from the latter.

The night of the 6th was long and wearisome as I tossed about sleeplessly, mindful that for both of us our chances of reaching succour were now slipping silently and relentlessly away. The morning of 7 January opened with better weather. In view of the seriousness of the position it had been agreed overnight that at all costs we would go on in the morning, with Mertz in his bag strapped on the sledge. It was therefore a doubly sad blow that morning to find that my companion was again touched with dysentery and so weak as to be quite helpless. Later in the afternoon he became delirious, talking incoherently. About midnight he appeared to doze off to sleep and with a feeling of relief I slid down into my own bag, not to sleep, though weary enough, but to get warm again and to think matters over. After a couple of hours, having felt no movement, I stretched out my arm and found that my comrade was stiff in death. He had been accepted into 'the peace that passeth all understanding'.

Dr Xavier Mertz, who died of starvation and cold after Ninnis's sledge was lost in the crevasse

ALONE

Outside the bowl of chaos was brimming with drift-snow as I lay in the sleeping-bag beside my dead companion. There appeared to be little hope of reaching the Hut, still one hundred miles away. It was easy to sleep in the bag, and the weather was cruel outside. Late that evening, the 8th, I took the body of Mertz, still toggled up in his bag, outside the tent, piled snow

blocks around it and raised a rough cross made of the two discarded halves of the sledge runners. Before retiring to rest in the evening I read through the burial service. 10 January arrived in a turmoil of wind and thick drift. The start was still further delayed.

The next day, 11 January, a beautiful calm day of sunshine, I set out over a good surface. From the start my feet felt curiously lumpy and sore. They had become so painful after a mile of walking that I decided to examine them on the spot, sitting in the lee of the sledge in brilliant sunshine. I had not had my socks off for some days for, while lying in camp, it had not seemed necessary. On taking off the third and inner pair of socks the sight of my feet gave me quite a shock, for the thickened skin of the soles had separated in each case as a complete layer, and abundant watery fluid had escaped saturating the sock. The new skin beneath was very much abraded and raw. Several of my toes had commenced to blacken and fester near the tops and the nails were puffed and loose. I smeared the new skin and the raw surfaces with lanoline, and then with the aid of bandages bound the old skin casts back in place, for these were comfortable and soft in contact with the abraded surface. Over the bandages were slipped six pairs of thick woollen socks, then fur boots. Then on I went, treading rather like a cat on wet ground endeavouring to save my feet from pain. By 5.30 p.m. I was quite worn out, though having covered but six and a quarter miles. The day following passed in a howling blizzard and I could do nothing but attend to my feet and other raw patches.

17 January was another day of overcast sky and steady falling snow. A start was made at 8 a.m. I was hauling the sledge through deep snow up a fairly steep slope when my feet broke through into a crevasse. I shot through the centre of the bridge in a flash, but the latter part of the fall was decelerated by the friction of the harness ropes which, as the sledge ran up, sawed back into the thick compact snow forming the margin of the lid. Having seen my com-

ades perish in diverse ways and having lost hope of ever reaching the Hut, I had already many times speculated on what the end would be like. So it happened that as I fell through into the crevasse the thought 'so this is the end' blazed up in my mind, for it was to be expected that the next moment the sledge would follow through, crash on my head and all go to the unseen bottom. But the unexpected happened and the sledge held, the deep snow acting as a brake.

In the moment that elapsed before the rope ceased to descend, delaying the issue, a great regret swept through my mind, namely, that after having stinted myself so assiduously in order to save food, I should pass on now to eternity without the satisfaction of what remained. Realising that the sledge was holding I began to look around. The crevasse was somewhat over six feet wide and sheer walled, descending into blue depths below.

Above at the other end of the fourteen-foot rope, was the daylight seen through the hole in the lid. In my weak condition, the prospect of climbing out seemed very poor indeed, but in a few moments the struggle was begun. A great effort brought a knot in the rope within my grasp, and, after a moment's rest, I was able to draw myself up and reach another, and, at length, hauled my body on to the overhanging snow-lid. Then, when all appeared to be well and before I could get to quite solid ground, a further section of the lid gave way, precipitating me once more to the full length of the rope. There, exhausted, weak and chilled, hanging freely in space and slowly turning round as the rope twisted one way and the other, I felt that I had done my utmost and failed, that I had no more strength to try again and that all was over except the passing.

It was the occasion for a supreme attempt. I applied myself to one last tremendous effort. The struggle occupied some time, but I slowly worked upward to the surface. This time emerging feet first, still clinging to the rope, I pushed myself out extended at full length on the lid and then shuffled safely on to the solid ground at the side. Then came the reaction from the great nerve strain and lying there alongside the sledge my mind faded into a blank.

When consciousness returned it was a full hour or two later, for I was partly covered with newly fallen snow and numb with the cold. I took at least three hours to erect the tent, get things snugly inside and clear the snow from my clothes. Between each movement, almost, I had to rest. Then reclining in luxury in the sleeping-bag I ate a little food and thought matters over. It was a time when the mood of the Persian philosopher appealed to me:

'Unborn To-morrow and dead Yesterday,
Why fret about them if To-day be sweet?'

I was confronted with this problem: whether it was better to enjoy life for a few days, sleeping and eating my fill until the provisions gave out, or to 'plug on' again in hunger with the prospect of plunging at any moment into eternity without the supreme satisfaction and pleasure of the food.

On the 19th it was overcast and light snow falling; very dispiriting conditions after the experience of the day before – but I resolved to go ahead and leave the rest to Providence. The sun at last appeared on the 19th, and the march was resumed by 8.30 a.m. At length the glacier was crossed and the tent pitched on a snowy slope. I had never dared to expect to get so far and now that it was an accomplished fact I was intoxicated with joy.

20 January was a wretched overcast day, and I covered two and a half miles. High wind and dense driving snow persisted. Torrents of snow fell throughout the 25th and it sizzled and rattled against the tent under the influence of a gale of wind. Only four pounds of food remained now and there was no guarantee that the weather would clear in the near future, so the position was most anxious. At that time the skin was coming off my hands, which were the last parts of my body to peel. A moulting of the hair followed the peeling of the skin. Irregular tufts of

Memorial to Lt Ninnis and Dr Mertz

beard came out and there was a general shedding of hair from my head, so much so that at each camp thereabouts the snowy floor of the tent was noticeably darkened.

On the 26th, the wind blowing from behind, the travelling was rapid. After covering nine miles I was thoroughly done up. As the 27th was just such another day as the 26th I decided to rest further. On 28 January the evening turned out beautifully fine and my spirits rose to a high pitch, for I felt for the first time that there was a really good chance of making the Hut. The change in the weather had come most opportunely, for there now remained only about twenty small chips of cooked dog meat in addition to half a pound of raisins and a few ounces of chocolate which I had kept carefully guarded for emergencies.

After several hours' march the surface changed from snow to slippery ice. I could scarcely keep on my feet at all, falling every few moments and bruising my emaciated self until I expected to see my bones burst through the clothes. Before giving up, I even tried crawling on my hands and knees. However, the day's run, fourteen miles, was by no means a poor one.

Having erected the tent I set to work to improvise crampons. With this object in view the theodolite case was cut up, providing two flat pieces of wood into which were stuck as many screws and nails as could be procured by dismantling the sledgemeter and the theodolite itself. In the repair-bag there were also still a few ice-nails. Late the next day, the wind which had risen in the night fell off and a start was made westwards over the ice slopes with the pieces of nail-studded wood lashed to my feet. The crampons were not a complete success for they gradually broke up, lasting only a distance of six miles.

A blizzard was in full career on 31 January and I spent all day and most of the night on the crampons. To have attempted the descent of the five and a half miles of steep ice slope to the Hut with such inadequate and fragile crampons, weak as I still was, would have been only as a last resort.

Whilst these preparations were in progress the wind slackened. At last the longed for event was to be realised. I set off. Before a couple of miles had been covered the wind had fallen off altogether, and after that it was gloriously calm and clear. I had reached within one and a half miles of the Hut. The long journey was at an end – a terrible chapter of my life was concluded.

Then the rocks around the winter quarters began to come into view; and lo there were human figures! They almost seemed unreal – was it all a dream? No, indeed, for after a brief moment one of them observed me and waved an arm – I replied – there was a commotion and they all ran towards the Hut. Minutes passed as I slowly descended trailing the sledge. Then a head rose over the brow of the hill and there was Bickerton, breathless after a long run uphill. I expect for a while he wondered which of us it was. Soon we had shaken hands. Five men had remained behind from our party. For myself that wonderful occasion was robbed of complete joy by the absence of my two gallant companions, and as we descended to the Hut there were moist eyes amongst the little party as they learnt of the fate of Ninnis and Mertz.

The long Antarctic winter was fast approaching and we turned to meet it with resolution.

ACKNOWLEDGEMENTS

The editor and publishers gratefully acknowledge the following
books and authors, upon which this collection is based:

My Flight to the Cape and Back
Sir Alan Cobham, K.B.E.
A. & C. Black Ltd
(*Permission kindly granted by A. Cobham*)

The Peking Battles Cape Horn
Captain Irving Johnson
Sea History Press
National Maritime Historical Society
(*Permission kindly granted by National Maritime Historical Society New York*)

Greenland Journey
Edited by Else Wegener
Blackie & Sons Limited
(*Permission kindly granted by Blackie & Son*)

Twenty Years Under the Sea
J. E. Williamson
John Lane The Bodley Head

The Assault on Mount Everest 1922
Brigadier-General Hon. C. G. Bruce, C.B., M.V.O.
Edward Arnold & Co
(*Permission kindly granted by The Mount Everest Foundation*)

Pearls and Savages
Captain Frank Hurley
G. P. Putnam's Sons

The Home of the Blizzard
Sir Douglas Mawson
Heinemann
(*Permission kindly granted by Alun Thomas, and The Mawson Institute*)

Every effort has been made to trace copyright holders, and to
attribute copyright correctly. The editor and publishers
wish to apologise for any errors or omissions, and would be
interested to hear from anyone not here acknowledged.